SPY THATCHER

SPY
THATCHER

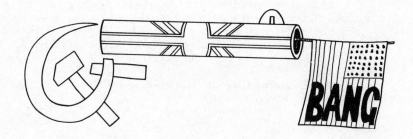

Edited by
WILLIAM RUSHTON

PAVILION
MICHAEL JOSEPH

First published in Great Britain in 1987 by
Pavilion Books Limited
196 Shaftesbury Avenue, London WC2H 8JL
in association with Michael Joseph Limited
27 Wrights Lane, Kensington, London W8 5TZ
Second Impression November 1987
Third Impression December 1987

Text and illustrations © William Rushton 1987

British Cataloguing in Publication Data
Rushton, William
    Spy Thatcher
    1. Great Britain——Politics and
    government——Anecdotes, facetiae,
    satire, etc.
    I. Title
    320.941′0207   JN231

    ISBN 1-85145-260-5

Printed and bound in Great Britain by
Billing and Sons Limited, Worcester.

PUBLISHER'S NOTE

All the characters in this book are unreal and bear little relation to anything living or dead.

SPYTHATCHER

'Down these mean streets a man must go who is not himself mean – who is neither tarnished nor afraid. He must be a complete man and a common man and yet an unusual man. He must be a man of honour, by instinct, by inevitability, without thought of it and certainly without saying it. He will take no man's money dishonestly and no man's insolence without a due and dispassionate revenge.'

Raymond Chandler
The Simple Art of Murder

EDITOR'S NOTE

This all came as a great surprise to me. I was walking quietly down Filth Street in Soho, having just been to the offices of *Private Eye* to collect the brown envelope that they slip me monthly and will so long as I still have the negatives, when I thought I saw my old friend and colleague, Auberon Waugh, the distinguished editor of *Literary Review*, the finest literary magazine in the World in my view, slipping through the multicoloured and distinctly tacky plastic strips that curtain the entrance to 'The Hot-Bed', a 24-hour drinking parlour for Maltese businessmen. Auberon Waugh is distinctly recognisable from the rear: the wide-brimmed Herbert Johnson hat, the pin-stripe suit – you don't see much of that in the Soho area. I followed him in, thinking how deeply embarrassed he would be when discovered in this low 'boîte'. It took some little time for my eyes to grow accustomed to the sudden gloom – and indeed my feet to the rising damp – but at last I spotted the familiar figure at the bar.

'Hello, you old bastard!' I cried, slapping him on the back, to find myself peering into the wild eyes of a large black man. I apologised immediately and explained the case of mistaken identity. I offered him a drink. He had a large brandy and I, now alas teetotal, a glass of flat Perrier water. The bill, as I remember came to £78.43. Anyway, the upshot of all this was my friend revealed himself to be a senior diplomat from a country on the Ivory Coast, which apparently had made many representatons to Mr Waugh, requesting him to accept the Kingship. They apparently worship him there, so he was quite delighted to be mistaken for the Once and Future King.

'You meet some interesting people here' he replied, when I enquired what he was doing drinking in such a sink. I couldn't see any, but as I excused myself and aimed for the lavatories, I fell full-length on the dank carpet over the recumbent form of another customer.

'Now *he* is interesting' said my new friend. 'He was a big man in Intelligence. Your MI5, no less, no more. He has retired and taken to the strong bottle. My word, he has a tale to tell.'

Some old instinct seemed to awaken within me. It's years since I beat a scoop out of some poor fool, or stuck my foot in the door of a shivering widow, but the old hackles were a-quiver.

'What would you like to drink?' I shouted at the corpse. Eat your heart out, Lazarus, he was primed and ready on a bar-stool before I reached the question-mark.

'Pink gin' he beamed.

The totally nude barmaid had never heard of Angostura, but my friend the diplomat had a bottle of Bitters in his brief-case.

'My name is Jesmond Barker' said Jesmond Barker, rattling his now empty glass on the bar. 'Oh, thank you,' he said when I volunteered to replenish it. The diplomat had another large brandy. This time the bill went into three figures. I wondered idly as I wrote out a cheque to 'Maltese Smallholdings (Switzerland) Inc.' how Jesmond Barker could afford to drink in such a place.

'I don't drink here' he said. 'I only came in to lie down for a while.'

He saw my look of amazement.

'It's cool and dark and safe. Our friend here is the bouncer.'

The large black man smiled. 'There is not all that much money in diplomacy, but it is capital for a bouncer to have CD plates.'

'Who are you then?' asked Barker. 'I like to know the name of those who buy me large pink gins, and their occupation.'

I told him both.

'Aha!' he said. 'You write a little, you say. You were doubtless blessed with an education. I was not. Otherwise I could tell the tale I have to tell. Nail the bastards once and for all. Another pink gin, Doris, and put your clothes on, your boils are oozing. Are you a man who can be trusted, Rushbag? Are you? Want to write the book that does for all of them, not like that bloody man Wright? All that sodding publicity in Australia. Have you *read* that book?'

We both shook our heads.

'Nor have I, and I won't. It'll be all self-justification, and Who's a Clever Boy Then? and page after page of Practical Wireless for the Criminally Insane.'

I bought Barker another large pink gin. Lavender Portakabin, for that was the name of the diplomatic bouncer or bouncing diplomat, made his excuses and left, his place in history guaranteed.

'All I want to do, old boy,' whispered Barker, in my ear, 'is make enough money to get me to Australia. Far from the maddening bastards. Somewhere where Colonel Balls can't get me with his Exocet. You don't know Colonel Balls, do you? He'll know you, by now, I should think they're going through your file at the Registry e'en now, as we speak, as we order another round of gins, they'll be checking you out. Running you through the computer. Who's that bearded bugger with Barker in the basement? That big darkie, he's one of them, mark my words. Why do you think he keeps the pink stuff in his briefcase, eh? There are no coincidences in the Secret World. Come on, Doris, fill the flowing bowl. A right tart, our Doris. Never give a broker an even suck, that's her motto. I can tell you things, Rushbag, that will turn your bushy beard white. Are you game? You know some dam' fool publisher who'd jump at the chance, eh? Fat advance, Concorde to Wagga Wagga, raise wombats or such in the Land of Freckle-backed Women. No country that produces Clive James and Rolf Harris and Rupert Murdoch can be all good, can it? Be fair. Fat advance, a hide-out in the Cotswolds, I'll blab, you write, bags of pink gin for inspiration, loosen the inhibitions, out comes the book, and run like hell. And as for Maggie, I would be highly delighted if the silly bitch would drag me before the Beak, slap injunctions all over the place, and make me a millionaire.'

'When would you like to start?' I asked.

'Now' he said. 'This minute. Before the computer spews out

9

your evil-doings and the Watchers in the Black Van arrive. Come. Farewell, Doris, there's an old Arabian proverb – may your camels mate and prosper, and bear fruit incessantly, but not in your living-room. Always leave them, Rushbag, shouting for less.'

I found a taxi outside, and whispered to the driver, 'Pavilion Books.'

★   ★   ★

We started work in the Cotswolds three days later. It was a quaint little hotel, deliberately so, but quiet in Autumn, and blessed with Room Service. I would start the day with the Continental Breakfast and a lot of coffee. Barker would commence on *The Times* crossword and the Pink Gin. 'Driven to it,' he would say, 'by pressure, and deceit, and the sheer fucking magnitude of the plot.' After breakfast, we would begin, and work through non-stop, except for short breaks when Mrs Porringer appeared from below with coffee and Pink Gins, until dinner. After three days, I became convinced that I was as mad as he. I would join him in the morning combing the room for bugging devices, peering through binoculars at the distant hills in case Colonel Balls should appear over the horizon with a shooting party. On the fourth day, Barker was very jumpy, 'They can usually find you in four days, five at most, wherever you are. I think we should move.' I agreed wholeheartedly, and nearly soiled my tweeds when a charabanc drew up full of compost-salesmen on their way to a seminar in Bath.

We drove North, and found a decent little Commercial Hotel on the Wirral, with a licence. There we stayed and worked for another three days, before setting off again, this time for the Cairngorms. By now, I was as paranoid as Barker. The work became more and more difficult, I was constantly asking him to lower his voice, that was at times far too loud for comfort, given the sophisticated nature of bugging today. He became more and more incoherent and it was always extremely difficult to capture his gist with my appalling shorthand. After three months of this, we finished the final chapter closely closeted in a bathroom on Alderney, with all the taps running.

The last I saw of him was at Charles de Gaulle Airport – we had hovered from the Channel Islands and taken a week to reach Paris in a variety of vehicles and disguises. The devious route he had booked to Australia involved all five continents over and over again. He even arrived in and left Australia twice before he set down for the last time some two months later.

'Be wary, Rushbag' he said. 'Watch the rooftops. Watch your back. Never get caught with your trousers down. They'll take you any way they can. A dirigible may fall on you, it's been known. The pavement may open up beneath you. A passing Dachsund may explode. Your toothpaste may contain *curare*. Remember, there is *no-one* you can trust. So long, old fruit, and good luck to you!' And he was gone. I have received one postcard from him from Anchorage, wishing that I was there. As far as I know he is sitting in Australia, surrounded by wombats or whatever, waiting for the writs.

I remember saying to him one evening over dinner as we talked of Australia, that he would, while being as far away from MI5 as was possible, be perilously close to his old antagonist, Wright.

'Rushbag' he said. 'I was perilously close to Wright for twenty-five or more years, and only met him once. It's all part of the plot.'

And what a plot. If half of what he says is true, we live in deeply worrying times. I have read Wright's book, Barker always refused to, and there seems to be a common thread, the cast is much the same, the events are similar, though their chronology seems awry, but time has obviously played tricks on both of them. Both have axes to grind, and I would read both books, if you are ever allowed to, with equal pinches of salt. If either book reveals facts that a Government would prefer to have us not know, then I would have thought that they were precisely the facts that we should know.

Getting his book into some semblance of order was a massive task, and I still live in constant fear of assassination – I received a polite phone-call asking about my health from Colonel Balls, which caused me to shiver uncontrollably for a week. But I am now, I must confess, as a result of meeting Barker, a fervent disciple of The Great Conspiracy Theory. They *are* everywhere! Watch Out!

William Rushton
EDITOR

PROLOGUE

'For years I have wondered what the last day would be like. In January 1976, after two decades in the top echelons of the British Security Service, MI5, it was time to rejoin the real world.'*

The opening words of Peter Wright's book scudded through my addled brain as I myself emerged for the final time from Euston Road tube station, wishing that I had had sufficient energy and time to read the rest of it, but that had been quite enough. Suffice to say those two sentences were sufficient to inspire me to jump on the bandwagon. If that's the sort of thing the public want, then I am more than happy to come out of the cold, or the closet, or wherever. I made a note on my cuff in invisible ink to find a publisher before I set off Down Under to grow wombats near Wagga Wagga.

Smiling at the thought of the huge advance and litigation to come, I quickly jumped onto an omnibus, heading north. Surreptitiously I removed my false moustache and dropped it in the used ticket slot. Quickly I put on dark glasses and a tartan cap with bobble and jumped off as the conductor approached. I hailed a taxi travelling south. 'Heathrow!' I shouted, though I

---

* The fact that you have read this makes you an accessory after the fact, and liable to imprisonment in the Tower. Bad luck. Now read on.

added quietly through the glass partition, 'Make that Charing Cross Station.' On arrival, I darted through the station and crossed the bridge to Waterloo, thence a train to Clapham Junction. A mini-cab took me then to East Putney, where I boarded the Underground to Earls Court. Finally, a taxi back to Gower Street. That should have shaken off any 'tail'. It would have been most foolish on my last day at 'The Office' to have given away its whereabouts. I entered the unmarked entrance in that anonymous office block that stands between an art college and a hospital. The HQ of British Counter-espionage.

I showed my pass to Sgt. Heinemann who has been at that desk in reception for more years than he can remember.

'Well, Heinemann' I said, 'quoth the Raven "Nevermore",' I quoted.

'What's the password?' he grunted. I had never ceased to be fascinated by the pointed lump on the right side of his totally bald head – a bullet that had passed through his brain at the Second Battle of Mons.

'Shirley Temple?' I suggested. I made for the lift. Heinemann was still a spritely man for his age and weight. He brought me down with a flying tackle round the thighs. My nose was caught in the muzzle of his service revolver.

'That was yesterday' he breathed heavily. 'Asshole.'

'I have it in my diary' I said.

'Don't count if you 'as to read it.' He had lived his life by the book. It had probably taken most of it to read it.

There we lay, gasping like beached herring. Then we heard the cheerful voice of the Director-General.

'Hello, and what are you two up to? Fun and games so early in the day!'

'This bugger don't know the password, sir.' Heinemann knelt at attention and saluted.

'Oh come along, Jesmond, it's easy. Even Heineman can remember it. Can't you Heinemann?'

'Sir Leonard Hutton' he beamed.

'There you are, Jesmond. Specially picked for your last day, knowing your love of the Noble Game.' He helped me to my feet. Heinemann was marching on his knees towards the wreckage of his desk. the Director-General and I entered the lift. I

14

pressed the button for the sixth floor.

'Good to see he's still keen as mustard' said the D-G. 'You'll be at the party tonight?'

'It *is* my farewell party, sir.'

'Good. Time you settled down. Any plans?'

'Australia, sir' I replied.

'Oh my God' he placed the ferrule of his umbrella on my Adam's apple. 'Not of a Literary bent, are we?'

'Oh, no, sir' I lied. The lift stopped, and we strode together down the corridor. My office was next to the Director-General's extensive suite. The offices hummed with the sound of senior spies working at *The Times* crossword puzzle. I unlocked my door. There before me were the essential tools of the Master Spy. A desk, a chair, two telephones, one scrambled, one lightly boiled, two pigeons, a large safe with massive locks, a hat-rack, a drinks cabinet and a large, nubile blonde woman, stirred and visibly shaken.

'Good morning, Miss Moneypenny' I said, and threw my cap nonchalantly at the hat-rack. It hit a pigeon and landed in the wastepaper basket. Once in 45 years would have been nice, I thought.

She wept openly. I patted her on the shoulder.

'Be a brave soldier, Miss Moneypenny' I said, 'there's work to be done. Warm up the shredder while I open the safe.' She kicked the starter, and the machine began to judder as I attacked the safe with my enormous bunch of keys. After almost ten minutes, I pulled the great door open. Files upon files. A vast accumulation of information and misinformation. Reports from agents the globe over. Rainfall in the Ukraine 1947. Hours of sunshine in Belfast 1973. Hours of cricket lost because of rain at Old Trafford 1965. I had never lost my initial fascination for weather.

'Heigh ho, Miss Moneypenny' I said. 'Clean break. Everything goes.'

And we began to feed the files into the shredder, which, in turn, belched the spaghetti-like remnants into the burn bag. First the files, then the notes, the doodles, the diaries (Damn! I'd meant to keep them), then the desk, unscrupulous busy-bodies might read something from indentations of my heavier scribblings, acusations written perhaps in a fit of pique, blonde hairs, the hat-rack, the pictures on the wall – colleagues of mine in various disguises – some of my heroes; Winnie, King Farouk, Sir Gerald Nabarro, weatherman Jack Scott, Jerry Lee Lewis. Finally, the most difficult moment, for not only had she been my right hand for nearly twenty years, but she was now quite bulky, the shredding of Miss Moneypenny. I kissed her warmly, and wished her well, and then rang down to Heinemann to fetch the bag. The office was quite empty.

I went downstairs to the Establishments Office. I handed in my keys, my book of Passwords, some false noses, a mackintosh with inbuilt hump, a large number of plastic cards that had gained me admission to assorted rooms, closets and cupboards. My unlimited access to the Great Secrets of our nation was ended. I signed several documents to do with the Official Secrets Act left-handed with fingers crossed, and also unremarked by the Assistant Head of Establishments, with an assumed name.

It was now time to leave the World of Espionage forever. I made my way downstairs (I had handed in my key to the lift), tip-toed past the snoozing form of Sgt. Heinemann and stepped out into Gower Street for the last time. It was drizzling. I cursed the fact that I had shredded my Burberry, and lost half my umbrella poking in the last bits of Miss Moneypenny. I took a taxi over to MI5's offices at the top of Curzon Street. A good deal of midnight oil had burnt here, wrestling with the Great Conspiracy Theory. Out of Philby, Burgess, Maclean, Blunt and Hollis, and leading in the most unlikely directions, if my solution is correct. Perhaps I will never know.

I went into the club bar. The MI5 Hierarchy had officially planned a surprise party for me, but news about it had been in *The Times* Diary next morning, so now it was an Official Farewell Party and embossed invitations had gone out. This had apparently caused some confusion in the ranks: some came in full evening dress with decorations, some in fancy dress, Pierrot and Pierrette, a Dick with his Pantomime Cat, and the Director-General as a Colonel in the Bengal Lancers which he had been, so he fell neatly between the two camps. He made a pretty little speech, and presented me with an Antique Digital Clock, suitably inscribed 'To You. From You Know Who For You Know What'. Then Lord Clandestine, who I thought was dead, stood up and said that my parting was such sweet sorrow that he would have to sit down again. I rang for a taxi to take me to Heathrow. It dropped me at Charing Cross Station. My career was over. Sweet sorrow indeed.

Father and Colonel Balls.

1

It all began in 1949. The weather was absolutely terrible, but then it always is in Espionage, fact or fiction. I was on Salisbury Plain, and it was pissing down. It rains a good deal in Shakespeare too, come to think of it. I spent my days out in the open with my balloons, carrying out vital experiments for the London Rubber Company. I had been trying for years to come up with a weather balloon that could withstand a bolt of lightning. It was damned hard work. That day, as I say, I was out on the Plain and the climate was perfect for research. Thunder rolled and lightning flashed. I had three balloons up and they seemed to be withstanding all that Mother Nature could throw at them. My field telephone rang. It was my father, Neville Barker, and it occurred to me as he introduced himself, that I had never had the faintest idea what he did for a living. I suppose other people's fathers may be something of a mystery to them, but all I could say of my father, having known him many years, was that he kept pigeons and drank to excess.

'Charlie Orange wants to see us' he said.

I had met Orange, of course. He was an old friend of father's. Father had often told me that they had worked together in the war, and then always changed the subject, or repaired to the cupboard under the stairs for another bottle. I had no clue as to what Father had done in the war. I never met him during that period. I had spent the war years somewhere on the South Coast – such was the security I never did discover where, researching and building barrage balloons – hence my work for London Rubber. I can say, with hand on heart, and with no feeling of immodesty that there was no man in the world who understood the balloon as well as I. And very few I would bow to as my superior, outside Japan, who were my master with the kite.

'What about?' I asked.

'Aha' said Father, mysteriously. That is precisely what he would say before the war when he set off on one of his 'trips'. He would be standing at the garden gate, suitcase in hand, wearing sometimes a fur hat with ear-pieces, sometimes a solar topee.

'Where are you going, Daddy?' I would ask.

'Aha' he would say, and set off for the bus-stop.

'I'll pick you up at your digs tomorrow morning' he said. 'Wear a tie.'

He had rung off before I had time to find out more.

It was a typical English Spring day as we drove to London next morning in a steady drizzle and parked in Petty France. Father dragged me through St James' Park Station, in and out of the Army and Navy Stores ('Good shop' he said. 'They understand a camel-load.') back through the station and then into a large Victorian block overlooking the Park.

'Can't be too careful' he said. 'You never know.'

I hadn't been in London for some time. Indeed the last time I had been up in town it was V-J night. A night of endless celebration, song, dance and watery beer, and a buxom girl from Wimbledon as I recall, though, alas, her name escapes me – if I ever knew it. It was the last and only happy time that I entered an Air-Raid Shelter. She took me to heights that even I, a practised balloon-man, found dizzying. But then again, I have always been a martyr to vertigo.

'Dirty little bugger' muttered my Father. How had he guessed? I was wearing my baggiest corduroys. And, incidentally, a tie.

We were in a large waiting-room, and not the first to arrive. There were a number of men in uniform, others that I guessed were scientists from the stains on the fronts of their pin-stripes and two men in the corner in wide, black hats peering at us inquisitively through holes in their newspapers. They both wore dark glasses.

'Spies, eh?' I whispered to Father, more in jest.

'Mum's the word' he snapped, and waved to the strange duo.

'You must be the Barkers,' a small red-faced man, with moustaches that might have served at Waterloo, barked at us from below. 'I am Colonel Gascoyne Balls from the War Box. Welcome aboard. Well done. Your Country Needs You. Drinky?'

My father nodded eagerly, and the Colonel signalled to a white-coated servant who came over with a trayful of pink gins. My father drank three in quick succession, and seemed to relax. He belched quietly in my ear.

'Absolutely right, old boy. Spies to a man.'

My brain was racing. It did in those days, it hadn't been addled, washed or damaged. Everything fell into place.

'Good God, father' I whispered. 'You're in the Secret Service.'

'Man and boy' he replied. He took another couple of gins from a passing tray. He winked at me. 'All part of the plot, old fellow, all part of the plot.'

'But why am I here?' I enquired, gesturing at the brass.

'Jobs for the boys, old boy' he replied. 'Time you stopped farting about on Salisbury Plain. Get down to Spy-Thatching.'

'Thatching?' I said, wondering if the pink gins were talking.

'Ancient and honourable craft, Jesmond, thatching shpiesd.'

I would have enquired further but Charlie Orange appeared through one half of large double-doors and ushered us into a long, bright room with conference table and chairs. We all had blotters labelled 'TOP SECRET' and rolled-gold propelling pencils inscribed 'The Blue Train'.

Charlie Orange rose and beamed at us. 'Most of you know me. Charlie Orange, Ministry of Defence. I certainly know all about you.'

I was the only person to laugh politely. Orange looked at me over the top of his spectacles. 'Air Raid Shelter. V-J Day. Laura Porter. 43, The Glebe, Orpington.'

I blushed vigorously, and made a note of her name and address on my blotter.

'The Country' continued Orange, 'is, to put it mildly, up Shit

Creek and there's not a lot we can do about it. Not a paddle to be had. However the Powers That Be, the bloody Socialists, the bloody Reds, have, since Johnny Russki blockaded Berlin, decided that pro tem they're on our side. I have had no less a person than the Prime Minister, Clement bloody Attlee, Public School man ought to know better, you can excuse fat oiks like Bevin and Bevan, but Clement bloody Attlee I ask you – anyway I have had him on the telephone in some agitation. Silly little prick. What did I think? I think, quoth I, Prime Minister (pause to spit) that we are at war, and I remembered rather a felicitous phrase, coined I believe by my good lady, a *Cold* War and we'd better bloody do something about it. So, the upshot was I was handed the unenviable task of co-ordinating the activities of you spies, and Intelligence Men, Officers, Gentlemen and Boffins and, in a manner of speaking, going to war.'

He paused for effect, sipped at his Gin and waved away some light applause.

'I did this sort of thing in the last one. Turned a bizarre rag-bag gathering of academics, authors, boffins, baggy-nosed comedians, and God-knows-what into a tight, cohesive unit that armed with paper-clips, gum and paste, rubber bands and cake-tins won the bloody war virtually single-handed. At times I didn't know if I was in charge of the SOE or ENSA, but, by God, it worked! Now, the problem for us all to solve is simple – to find out what the stinking Reds are up to – we need Intelligence and you are it, Gentlemen. Any ideas?'

He began to talk to us individually and in pairs about eavesdropping techniques, the absolute necessity to know what the Russians and their satellites are talking about in their Embassies.

'Barker, you may wonder why you're here' he said to me. 'I want to try and marry your ballooning techniques with some sort of listening device. We may be able to float above them and hear what the bastards are up to. I want you to work with a man currently attached to the Services Electronics Research Laboratory. He's over there. It will be part-time work, of course, this experimentation. Don't give up your day job.' Orange was moving me across the room by the elbow. 'There won't be any pay, as such. Love of Country, eh? Here he is. Have a chat. Exchange telephone numbers. Jesmond Barker meet Peter Wright. Wright – Barker.'

Later, as I carried Father out into Birdcage Walk, I felt strangely excited. Though weather would doubtless remain a lifetime interest I had never really seen it as a lifetime's work. This was more like it. I was to tread in my Father's steps. Follow him into what I now realised was the family business – Espionage. I threw him into the back of a taxi and shouted his address. I was off to Orpington. In Father's immortal words, 'You never know.'

Myself with Fenton, my Siamese Twin Brother.

2

Years after I had joined the Service and had been given the plastic card that gained me unlimited access to the files, I made a point of seeking out those files relating to my father's career. What an extraordinary life he had led. The more I read the more I began to understand the long absences and the heavy drinking. He had, over a long period, infiltrated nearly every Secret Service on earth, including the KGB, the CIA, and quite by accident as it transpired, the French. He always employed the same technique, one that became extremely popular in fiction. It would be leaked to the target nation that he was disillusioned with the British Secret Service, and he would be seen lurking furtively outside their Embassy, bottle in hand. He would be seen in low bars, stiff with cheap drink. Finally he would be found face down in the gutter in the country selected. They never tortured him, as he would make it clear from the offset that he had a very low pain threshold. He would then spread disinformation, but such was his transparent honesty and charm that his interrogators could only believe his every word. In the course of these exchanges he would obviously pick up a good deal of information of value to our side. In time, he would be returned home as a 'double-agent'. One problem was that his interrogation would involve a large amount of drinking as his hosts fed or rather poured out his habit. This naturally made it very difficult for him to remember anything.

I read in one file how in a long session with a General close to the Kaiser he was given the entire German scenario for World War One, only to wake some hours later prostrate in the Unter den Linden, his mind a total blank.

His involuntary recruitment by French Intelligence was caused when, *en route* to Turkey, he fell, quite insensible, from the Orient Express a few miles outside Paris.

What effect did all this have on the child Jesmond? I was born the sickliest half of Siamese Twins. We were joined at the buttock, my brother and I, and sad to relate, never got on. We were so different. He, so muscular, athletic and thick as two short planks. Myself, a pathetic addendum on the Field of Play, but useful to have about when there was homework to be done. Our schooling was erratic. It would scarcely have lent credence to fathers 'defections' had we been seen to be carrying on as normal. Indeed as I realised in retrospect we had to be seen to suffer from his absences.

Thus, we started out at quite a decent Preparatory school, where we shared the honours academically. It's hard to accuse a twin of cheating, my brother would simply claim any signs thereof to be the result of that extraordinary telepathy that is said to exist between twins. The honours were not shared on the Rugby field and Cricket pitch. Fenton, my brother, was in both the XV and the XI. So was I in a manner of speaking. He was twice my size, and wore me like a haverbag, I suffered greatly for his sporting achievements. At cricket, I seemed to be nothing more than extra padding; at Rugby I was the one they punched and kicked. I was almost grateful when Father went off on one of his trips. (Bulgaria, I gathered later from the files.)

In no time at all Mother had to remove us from Prep school, and we were sent to an appalling local establishment where, at least, to my intense relief, there was less emphasis on sport, and I began to grow a little healthier.

Father came home and for a while things looked up. There was talk of our going to a minor public school. Then he was off again (Sweden in fact) and once again we were in the hands of the State, who could barely wait to get rid of us at fifteen. Fenton had become a brute and a bully, and announced that he intended to join the Army as a career. I was in no position to disagree.

Doubts, quite properly in my view, raised at the medical were quickly put to rest by Fenton's obvious ability to cope with anything they threw at him, regardless of my discomfiture. I almost drowned as he completed the Assault Course in record time. I have been deaf in my left ear ever since he scored maximum points on the Rifle Range. I was written off as a non-malignant growth. Whatever privations I suffered as Fenton ruthlessly pursued a glittering career in the Infantry were as nothing compared to those I underwent when Fenton discovered Sex. I know now how it would feel to go over Niagara Falls in a barrel. I would simply be thrust into a pillow-case with a book – I was still keenly pursuing my interest in Meteorology – but as passions mounted it became increasingly difficult to concentrate on isobars and warm fronts. As Fenton and his victim (I always thought of them as such) writhed and rolled I would be hurled into the air and whip-lashed onto the other side of the couple. There were beastly occasions when, close to suffocation, my face pressed into a page of cloud formations, I would be underneath the rutting couple.

Rather half-heartedly I suggested that I would very much like to go to University to read Weather, and qualify for some sort of career myself. The only other talent I possessed was an extraordinary dexterity with kites. This I practised while Fenton slept. Did I tell you that Fenton always insisted on sleeping outdoors? Hardiness and insensitivity, in addition to the brutishness and bullying. No small wonder I was miserable. My University ambitions were immediately pooh-poohed. Fenton was now a Captain in the Duke of Relwick's Mounted Foot, and he was older than I (technically) and larger (considerably). And, war loomed.

Indeed, before I could appeal to Father who reappeared briefly, tired, tanned and virtually incapable of putting two words together without falling over, war broke out again. Father was off (Berlin this time, where he did much to disrupt their experiments with Heavy Water) and in no time at all Fenton and I were on the beach at Dunkirk, awaiting evacuation. I was cleaning his boots (the most obvious role for me from the start had been to be Fenton's batman, and this I had been for his Army career to date) when my life suddenly and violently and for the first time changed for the better. It was a

Stuka bomber, diving low and strafeing the beach, that achieved what Medical Science had always been so loathe to attempt, separating Fenton and me for good. And how good! And how strange! Not to be tottering on tip-toe. To breathe air unsullied by Fenton's virulent armpit. Not to be someone else's baggage. To be free. After a remarkably short stay in a hospital near Basingstoke, I was quickly employed in research into barrage balloons for the Royal Air Force, and fascinating work it was. And when that was done, this expertise, allied to my knowledge of British Weather, led to my transfer to the Meteorological Department, and further success. I can claim, with all modesty, that it was I who persuaded General Eisenhower, against his better judgement, to chance his army on June 6th, 1944.

I remember feeling a keen sense of loss when the war ended. Perversely perhaps, I felt no sense of loss whatsoever when Fenton, whose career had hastened downhill rapidly without my brains at his right armpit, shot himself.

I went to work for the London Rubber Company.

The Kensington Gardens Caper.

3

A month after our meeting, the worst June in living memory according to my records, Wright telephoned me. He had the basis of a plan to get a listening device into the Russian Embassy. I became more and more excited as he outlined it to me. What he asked of me fell well within my bailiwick as it simply involved hovering a kite or balloon over the Embassy itself. For his own part he seemed confident that he could come up with the necessary hardware. It certainly looked as if we would soon be privy to current Russian thinking.

'We must experiment at once' he said. 'I have applied for a fortnight's use of an old Artillery Range on the Gower Peninsular.' I had never been to Wales. My word, these were exciting times.

We were to meet at Paddington Station next morning.

'Dress garishly' he said. 'We are Variety Artistes on our way to an engagement at the Old Alhambra, Tenby. A trunk will be delivered to you shortly with the name of our Act stencilled upon it. Cloke and Dagger. Rather good I thought.' That was the only time I ever heard him laugh. In the main he was a gloomy bugger.

I met him next morning by Platform Six. He looked very good. He had a green bowler hat, a bright yellow bow-tie which he revealed to me later, swivelled and lit up, a black-and-white checked suit and red patent leather shoes. He smoked a large cigar and seemed rather disappointed at my turn-out. I had ransacked my wardrobe and the best I could do was a baggy cap that father used to golf in, a brown tweed jacket, khaki shorts and sandals. My tie was, I thought, suitably garish. Blue with yellow spots – I think Fenton had bought it to impress one of his victims. I seem to remember him blind-folding me with it one grizzly evening in Soho.

'All right' said Wright. 'You can be the straight man. You are Les Dagger. I shall have to do the jokes.' He sighed deeply and ordered a porter to carry his large hamper to the train.

'My wife's gone to the West Indies' he said to the ticket-collector.

'Fuck her then' retorted the ticket-collector. I had no idea Wright was married.

★   ★   ★

We found a suitable Bed and Breakfast, relatively adjacent to the Range. We had successfully persuaded our landlady, Megan, she insisted that we call her, that we were a comic duo, briefly between engagements and keen, as many of our profession were, on ornithology. She promised us sandwiches and a flask of tea for our daily excursions.

'It's hard' she squawked in her rich Welsh way, 'look you, to think of you two gentlemen as theatricals.'

'Comedy is a serious business,' grunted Wright. And off we set, dragging the hamper full of equipment.

'So is Ornithology' said Megan, pointing to the hamper.

'We use it as a hide' I replied.

'Damned good' whispered Wright.

We did not need the full fortnight of experimentation, we hit pay-dirt on Day Three. The plan was simplicity itself. I would fly a kite over the Russian Embassy. It was close enough to Kensington Gardens not to raise any suspicions. From the kite a microphone would be suspended, which we would lower down an appropriate chimney. The sound would then come out – I'm not well-versed in the technical details of this operation – in some sort of wireless thing at one end and would be recorded by some sort of recording device. The kite would also act as an aerial, Wright told me.

On Day Three I must have been a good three hundred yards

from Wright who was in some old Sheep-shagger's Cottage. I hovered the kite above him, lowered the microphone and suddenly from the equipment behind me came his voice as clear as a bell.

'Hello, Barker. Hello Barker. Shout if you can hear me.'

'I HEAR YOU!' I shouted. 'ROGER AND OUT!'

He came running through the gorse towards me, as I retrieved the kite and microphone.

'We've cracked it' he said. 'All we need now is a little dressing. The equipment needs to be hidden when we're in Kensington Gardens. How?'

It was a ticklish problem, but I solved it. I could be disguised as a Nanny and the machinery could go in the perambulator.

'I'll be the Nanny' he said, 'in case of some malfunction.'

'If you like' I said. 'Perhaps I could be another nanny. We may need two prams.'

Wright nodded. 'We'll need some children about.'

'Dangerous things – children' I said. I'm terrified of them. Something to do with my own rude upbringing, I expect.

'I shall indent for some dwarfs. Colonel Balls can find anything at the drop of a hat. Levantine laundryman, Icelandic cricketers, Bedouin tribesmen who can speak fluent Mandarin. He knows them all.'

'When do we go?' I asked.

'That depends on Charlie Orange. I'll get him down here tomorrow to look at our work to date.'

Our Megan was deeply impressed next morning when a Daimler pulled up at her gate, and four men in bowler hats stepped out.

'Ooh, I think business is looking up for you Mr Cloke' she cooed from the window. 'These must be gentlemen from London I should think. I never thought they'd look so tasteful.' She peered out again through the net curtains. 'Are they *Agents* Mr Cloke?'

Wright stood up so quickly, his spectacles fell in his cup of tea.

'No, no, Megan, not at all! Banish all such thoughts from your mind, Megan. Things are not what they seem.' He turned to me, his face quite pale. 'My God, Barker' he hissed. 'She's on to us. It must be something *you* said or did. Bloody amateur.

There's been a leak. You, Barker, have leaked! Do something, you shit!'

Gently I placed my hands on his shoulders and restored him to his seat. I took his glasses out of the tea, cleaned them with his tie and replaced them on his nose. I kissed him lightly on the forehead.

'Forgive Mr Cloke' I said, joining Megan at the window. Orange and Company were coming up the path. 'These gentlemen are impressarios from the West End. The Hippodrome, the London Palladium, among others. Naturally Megan he is over-excited. They have come to see our act. It's nerves. This may or may not be the Big Time calling. Let them in, will you, Megan?'

She smiled in a most understanding manner, patted Wright on the head, and made for the front door. Charlie Orange came in first, removing his bowler hat with the suggestion of a bow to Megan who blushed. He was followed by a tall, stooped man I didn't recognise. The other two stayed outside, looking unnecessarily weary for the time and the place.

Wright had pulled himself together. He shook Orange warmly by the hand.

'Mr C.B. Cochrane, is it not?' he cried, winking viciously. 'And this would be Mr Jack Hylton, I imagine?'

Megan was beside herself. She has heard of those people, even in wildest Wales.

'Perhaps you'd like me to arrange the parlour for the show' she said. 'I could put some chairs in rows, and put red paper over the light, make it real theatrical.'

Wright's bow-tie was revolving again, and flashing. Mr C.B. Cochrane looked extremely lost and Mr Jack Hylton was studying the cracks in the ceiling.

'I could bring tea in the interval.' Megan seemed determined to have this World Premier in her parlour.

'Megan' I said, 'I think these gentlemen are accustomed to rather larger auditoria, and may, with respect, feel a little cramped indoors. I think we should take them out and – er – do the show right there.'

Everyone looked considerably relieved, and we all piled into the Daimler, shaking off Megan, who seemed intent on joining us, and drove to the Artillery Range.

The Demonstration went without a hitch, and Orange was highly impressed, particularly when we added our notion about the nannies, the prams and the dwarfs.

'Get your hampers and trunks,' he said. 'I'll drive you back to Town.'

'It's the Big Time' I whispered to Megan, as we departed.

'I'll see your names in lights, then' she smiled. There were tears in her eyes. I think she felt personally responsible for our success.

'My God, I hope not' said Wright. (Ha! Ha! Ha! in retrospect.)

★   ★   ★

Three days later, Wright telephoned me.

'We must meet at once.'

'Where?' I said.

'Where do you bloody think?' he snapped. 'St James's Park.'

I didn't know then that all meetings between those engaged in the Great Game take place in St James' Park amidst the pelicans and the muscovy ducks. It has been estimated that at any one time 73 per cent of those in the park are members of some branch of the Secret Service. I got that from Deighton in Catering. They are easily spotted. If you see any two men in formal wear drop their voices when passing a pelican, they are spies of some sort. (The legend still persists that the pelicans are wired for sound.)

I waited for Wright on the bridge. Big Ben vouched for his punctuality.

'Well, Barker, they're all jolly pleased with you so far' I blushed prettily. 'The balloon goes up on Monday. That gives us three days to organise our cover.'

We walked through the park, lowering our voices or changing the subject quickly as we passed other similar couples, who would flash a suspicious glance at us and also turn their volume down. It was not unlike being in some great open-air cathedral except, of course, for the ducks.

We discussed logistics. We were using Charlie Orange's Daimler to transport us to Kensington Gardens, a Ministry of Defence 'heavy' would be chauffeur. We had the two perambulators, one for Wright's receivers and recorder, the other for my paraphernalia. These would be camouflaged with woolly blankets and the suggestion of a sleeping baby's head, a pink hat with a bobble or somesuch.

'And Balls has come up with a couple of secure dwarfs', Wright announced, adding, 'How is your sister in Budleigh Salterton?' as a pelican erupted from a bush. He handed me a slip of paper. 'MI5 have a Safe Flat by the Albert Hall. We can change there. Details are all on this paper.' He hurdled a fence and made off into the trees.

'Do I have to eat it or anything once I've read it?' I shouted after him.

He couldn't have heard me.

★   ★   ★

It is hard to describe my feelings as I alighted from the bus at the Albert Hall that Monday morning. There was a heavy drizzle as I made my way to one of the Mansion blocks that surround the Concert Hall. I was very nervous certainly, but terribly excited. Had I been a crowd I would have buzzed. The 'chauffeur' opened the door to me, and I was ushered into what I imagined was the master-bedroom. My costume lay on the double-bed. Wright was already changed and sat at the dressing-table having make-up applied by a brutish-looking woman in a brown overall. There were two wigs set on the dressing table. I wondered if I was to be the blonde. The black curls and ringlets, with the touch of grey, seemed to be ideal for Wright, who looked very fine. I said as much. He thanked me curtly. I went into the bathroom to change. It somewhat tickled me to see that the false bosoms they had provided were stamped 'Property of H.M. Government'. I idly wondered which Department. They had clearly been worn before. I put on the grey uniform. It crackled with starch. What irony! I felt more manly, more military, in stiff grey with matching lisle stockings than I ever had in my ill-fitting khaki when I dangled from my brother's side at Aldershot and Dunkirk. I marched back into the bedroom and crashed to attention.

'Nurse Barker, reporting for duty!' I squawked, and saluted smartly.

Wright affected not to notice my little joke. The brutish make-up artist simply gestured me to the now vacant chair at the dressing–table. Some powder, a little lipstick, some colouring to the eyebrows, and in my view, at least, I looked rather pretty.

'Should turn a few heads in the Park' I said to Wright's reflection in the mirror.

'Oh, shut up' he said. What a miserable bugger. Perhaps it was nerves. The blonde wig did wonders for me. I put on the grey hat at a rakish tilt.

'Straighten that hat, you twerp!' ordered Wright. He looked the sort of Nanny that decent children might well wish to kill. He adjusted his own severe hat, and indicated with a nod that I should follow him.

The perambulators were in the hall, but Wright led me past them to a door which he unlocked. Our pair of dwarfs bounded out, dressed in little sailor suits. I supposed that from a distance they might pass muster, but from close to, they appeared middle-aged, and mildly debauched.

'OK' said Wright. 'You get these two little bastards down to the car. They can carry the kites. Lemmy and I will bring the prams. Right. Go!'

Lemmy, the 'chauffeur' as it transpired, dropped us at the bottom of the Broad Walk, that leads up from Kensington High Street to the Round Pond. In those days of course it was an avenue of fine elms. That was before the Dutch got at them with their filthy disease. We moved our motley caravan on to the expanse of grass that lies between the Walk and the road that leads to Kensington Palace. Through the trees we could see the roof of the Russian Embassy.

'No point in hanging about' said Wright. 'Get the kites aloft.'

It turned out not to be a day for kites. No matter what I did I could not get the kite to hang long enough over the Embassy, for Wright to even starting paying out the cable and lowering the microphone. We spent a frustrating half-an-hour, sometimes so near, but usually so far that on occasion I thought we might get entangled in something Royal at Kensington Palace, and attract the attention of the Parks Police. The dwarfs were getting pretty sick and tired of gambolling about, trying to appear thrilled to bits at our endeavours. (There was a nasty moment when some inquisitive old Memsahib, walking a small dog, asked the smaller of our duo how old he was? '58' replied the little fellow, and the old biddy tottered off towards the Round Pond, quite bemused. Wright gave him a sound cuff.)

'Plan 2, I fancy' I said to Wright. This meant the Weather-Balloon, a far sturdier beast. My 'baby's' body was a tank of hydrogen, and it took no time to inflate one of my balloons. The smaller dwarf, keen to crawl back into our regard, asked if he could inflate the other. All right, I said. Now we were in business. The balloon was up and hovering over the Embassy in minutes, and responding to my every adjustment. Wright began to pay out the cable, and in only two attempts, had lowered the microphone down one of the Embassy's larger chimneys. He went to his perambulator, and began to fiddle with various knobs.

'Hold this' I said to Lemmy, handing him the cable, and joined Wright. He was listening intently, bushy eyebrows wrestling. All I could hear was static. Suddenly he leaned deeper into the pram and said, 'Boogy! Boogy! Boogy!'

I thought that he'd probably gone mad. Then I realised that there was method in his apparently lunatic behaviour. Behind me was an elderly couple. They too had some sort of dog.

'Nasty afternoon for it' said she. She looked like a pudding.

'Now that's a balloon' said he. He looked like the dog, whatever that was.

'You've got a handful' said she. She was looking at the dwarfs who had now inflated the spare balloon, and with help from Lemmy, were hanging on to it for dear life.

Suddenly, there was a gabble of Russian from Wright's Pram.

'Icky! Bocky! Goo!' replied Wright.

'Listen to Baby!' she cackled.

This was a voluble Russian whose privacy we had invaded.

'Clever baby!' she laughed. 'What's he saying then?'

'There's a microphone hanging down the chimney' translated her husband, who, as chance would have it, spoke fluent Russian.

'What?' said she, incredulously. 'He was talking gobbledy-gook.'

'Did ickly boogy say Mikey-Mikey, Chimbley-Chimbley?' Wright was growing increasingly desperate.

'Baby was talking Russian' said the husband, 'and he was talking about a microphone hanging down his chimney.'

'Where would he have picked that up?' she enquired.

I missed any further discussion as I had run over to Lemmy and with his help was trying to lift the microphone out of the chimney. It was firmly stuck. More excited Russian boomed from the pram.

'What did baby say then, clever dick?' I heard her cry.

'Give us a hand, comrade, something is pulling it up' her husband replied.

Lemmy and I gave our end a tremendous yank, and up soared the balloon. It was free! Well, for a moment it was and then it caught in the chimney itself.

'Come on, Lemmy!' I cried 'Give it all you've got!'

He let go with one hand of the spare balloon, and with both hands on the cable he produced a prodigious heave. Up went the balloon again, taking a large part of the Embassy's chimney with it.

'That's awkward!' cried the wife, looking upwards.

'My, yes, you've got a problem there' the husband agreed, following her eye-line. The spare balloon was soaring heavenwards with both dwarfs dangling from it. They must have been strong little fellows for their ages – they were still hanging as they finally vanished into the clouds. Lemmy and I were ripped from our reverie by a series of dreadful sounds from Wright's pram. He was working feverishly at his equipment, barking out snatches of Brahms' Lullaby the while. Then there was a mighty explosion.

'Baby's gone bang' she said.

'Now the pram's on fire' said her husband.

'We never had children' she said.

'More trouble than they're worth' her husband nodded sadly.

Nanny Wright, wig akimbo, was racing his perambulator into the Round Pond, smoke and sparks still emanating from the half-submerged pram, while irate model-boat owners hurled abuse at him.

Lemmy and I melted away into the trees hand in hand. We were only starting to run for the car when we saw large men in overcoats approaching from the direction of the Russian Embassy.

I was most struck by how little of the incident was mentioned in the next morning's newspapers. Charlie Orange clearly had fingers in many newspaper-proprietors. There was no mention at all of Wright's night in Kensington Police Station.

4

Peter Wright never telephoned me again, so I imagined that my brief flirtation with MI5 was over. I continued to work quite happily at the London Rubber Company, but I was forced to admit to myself that I had thoroughly enjoyed the taste of adventure. Then one day in 1951 I received a telephone call from a man called Horse.

'Can we meet this afternoon?' he asked breathlessly.

We met on a park bench opposite the Foreign Office. He got straight to the point.

'What exactly do you do for us, Barker?' he asked. 'I found your phone number in the black book, but there's no record of your having worked for us.'

I described my one outing for MI5, placing as much blame as I could for the fiasco on Wright. I was sure that he'd done the same for me.

'Well' said Horse. 'I've been through the files, nary a mention of that. Not surprising, really. Sounds a bit of a cock-up. Bet you someone's put that file in the boiler. Wright, probably, he's up and coming, you know. Ambitious little shit, but he cracked that Russian bug in the Yank's Moscow Embassy.'

'Bully for him' I said. I really didn't want to know.

'Bloody Reds stuck it in the Great Seal of the United States on the wall behind the Ambassador's desk. Bloody cheek. The Americans couldn't work out how it worked so they got on to us. They called it 'The Thing'. Well, Wright cracked it. I won't bore you with the details – Wright will, he goes on for about three or four pages on the subject.'

'What?' I said. I was losing Horse's drift.

'Sorry' he said. 'Anyway, it was one in the eye for the Americans. They've been pissing themselves at our expense since the Burgess and Maclean business. So, currently, P. Wright is the Golden Boy. He's now working on the prototype of some great bugging device, involving a version of The Thing, a large suitcase and two umbrellas. Codename SATYR, if you must know.'

'But I mustn't know' I said. 'Must I?'

'Might as well' said Horse. 'You work for us, don't you?'

'Not really' I said.

'He'll be permanent shortly' sighed Horse, 'if they can come up with some way of paying him. He kept going on and on about how backward we were on the technical side, how we needed a scientist, and then this SATYR thing convinced them. We've got to keep ahead of the bloody Americans. That's the main thing. Roger Hollis, no less.' Horse noticed that I had no idea who he was talking about 'Deputy D-G' he explained. 'He said some very nice things about P. Wright and SATYR. P. Wright just said, "Condescending bastard" and went back to his hut. Still, charmless tit he may be, but he'll get on. Why don't you join up?'

'What as?' I said. I felt the Age of the Balloon was probably past.

'Any ideas?' said Horse.

'Not really' I said, shaking my head. Then I realised that he was pushing an unfinished *Times* crossword towards me.

'Oh' I said, adding quickly, 'That's WINDSOCK. That's ROUGH TRADE. Which gives you BELCH there, CACOPHONY, 8 across would be HENPECKED, 5 down therefore is CARNAL KNOWLEDGE. That leaves that fellow – "Saintly movement (5,4)".'

'Holy Shit!' said Horse.

'Good' I replied, 'but it doesn't fit.'

'No, what I mean is you're red-hot at the Puzzle. You've not seen this before?'

'No' I lied. It had taken all morning and lunchtime, and, tell the truth I hadn't quite finished it. Aha! 'MARKS TIME' I said. He looked at me in awe. 'Saintly movement' I said, marking time '*Saint Mark*'.

'Wow!' said Horse. 'Look, I'm going to fix up a lunch for you, me and Charlie Orange. You're our sort of chap, Barker.'

The lunch was arranged for the following Monday. I met Nigel Horse in St James' Park and we walked together through Green Park up into Piccadilly. We had walked almost half-way before Horse spoke.

'*En passant*' he said. 'You won't say a word to Charlie about all that Peter Wright stuff I told you last week, will you? We don't want him to think – ' He stopped. There was a heavy drizzle, I remember.

'What don't we want him to think?' I asked.

'We just don't want him to think' Horse replied. 'All right?'

'Fine with me' I said. And he did not speak again until we had entered Charlie Orange's Club – the In and Out. We were ushered into the Dining Room where Orange was already tucking into his second plateful of quails' eggs. He greeted us warmly and ordered. Over the Brown Windsor Soup he had ordered for me, he asked a little about my life history. In the main, people are quite interested in my period as a Siamese twin. Orange indicated no sign of interest, and it wasn't until he had ordered us all brandies that he turned to the purpose of his hospitality.

'Now, Barker, Nigel Horse here says you're the sort of chap we're looking for in MI5. What do you say to that?'

'Well,' I replied, 'I'm not certain in what capacity. I did thoroughly enjoy my one outing with Peter Wright in Kensington Gardens – I know it wasn't exactly a major success, but my disguise as a Nanny was jolly good.'

'What's he talking about, Nigel?' Orange leaned close to Horse, who whispered into his ear for some time.

'That *was* jolly good' said Orange. 'Knocked the Russki chimney off. Lot of rain got in. Gave em cause to pause.'

'Peter Wright burnt the file' I said. Horse began to look for something under the table. Orange took out a little notebook and jotted something down with an elegant gold fountain-pen.

'Clever that, Barker' he said, after a lengthy lull. 'Finding out about that. I won't ask you how you did it, but there's obviously more to you than meets the eye. I hear you are something of a wizard with *The Times* crossword.'

'I had plenty of time for that, sir, as a Siamese twin.'

'A Siamese twin, eh? Fascinating.' Now Charlie Orange leant in my direction. 'You're all right in my book. Join us full time.'

'I'd like to very much, sir' I replied 'Dare I ask about money?' Obviously I shouldn't have. They both looked at me as if I had just farted loudly during the Two Minutes Silence.

'Haven't you got a job?' asked Horse.

'Yes, with the London Rubber Company, but I'd have to give it up.'

'Point taken' said Orange 'Well, *we* haven't any money. More brandies?' Horse waved to an ancient waiter. Orange rambled on.

'The Treasury won't help, and, of course, as far as the Government are concerned, we MI5 chappies simply do not exist. We are not here. We are out there. We are a figment, which makes it damned difficult even if one asks them for the price of a cup of gin. I wonder if we could get you sponsored by Benson and Hedges or someone. Or a charity, perhaps? Are you mentally handicapped? You were physically handicapped as a child, of course. Is there a Home for Ex-Siamese twins or such?'

I shook my head, partly to show that it was in perfect working order.

'I wonder if the Army has any spare. Probably not. But, hang on, Jesmond Barker, what about the Air Ministry? You're a balloonist, aren't you?'

Horse coughed politely.

'Barker is rather good on weather, sir, as well. Doesn't that point to the Air Ministry Roof? Nobody'd ask questions.'

'Bloody brilliant!' roared Orange. 'Wonderful view, too. Well done, Horse! Any snags there, Barker?'

I had to confess to terminal vertigo, which wholly removed the wind from their sails.

'Good try, Nigel' said Orange, clearly furious. 'What about the Admiralty? Oh, God, no, they're coughing up for Wright, aren't they? Why can't you marry a rich widow, Barker? I did. It's a very small sacrifice to make for one's country.'

'There is also,' I said, 'the matter of a pension. You see the

London Rubber Company has an excellent scheme that – '

'My God!' cried Orange, causing several senior members to mutter. 'You may not live that long. You're money-mad, Barker. Oh, well, we'll just have to cut back on something.'

A waiter hovered. 'More brandies, sir?'

'No,' shouted Orange. 'Bugger off!' Horse coughed again.

'I'll have a word, sir, with Le Carré in Accounts. I'm sure we can come up with something.'

Orange seemed appeased. 'You'll have to go before a Board. Pure formality. In the meantime I'd like you to consider our Surveillance techniques. They're not very good. We have a lot of trouble with our Watchers – the blokes who follow Russian diplomats about. We seem to be falling down in that area. Any notions?'

'Well, not without knowing a little more about how you operate at the moment.'

'Can't tell you that' retorted Orange. 'That's Highly Classified. More than my job's worth. Good God!'

Lunch was over. Orange saw us to the door. He shook my hand quite warmly in the circumstances. I wouldn't blame him for having second thoughts about an ex-Siamese twin with vertigo.

'You'll have to trust us, Barker. We're not like those Civil Service fat cats. But there is always the secret vote. Now, there won't be any sort of contract between us, but if you do survive until pensionable age, I'm sure we'll be able to arrange something. We'll take care of you, Barker, I promise.'

I set off into Green Park, an altogether happier man. I was about to begin a new life in the shadows.

The Directorate.

5

Four days later I went to Leconfield House for my Selection Board. The frosted glass partition in the alcove slid back and it was the first time I ever met Heinemann. I was, of course rivetted by his lump. He, in turn, smelt my nervousness. He kept me waiting on the steps for a good twenty minutes while he telephoned Charlie Orange's office. There was a heavy drizzle, as I recall.

At last, he let me in. 'Come to see the D-G, have we, sweetie?' he cooed at me, displaying a mouthful of quite disgusting brown teeth. He marched me to the lift. It was a ridiculously old lift. As Heinemann operated the rope, he could have been Quasimodo, the Liftman of Notre Dame. We reached the Fifth Floor, the Heart of MI5. With considerable straining and grunting, and Quasimodo opened the grid iron gates. He led me down the corridor to the Director-General's Office. He shouted my name to a tweedy secretary with tidy moustaches. She picked up a red telephone. The size of this ante-room was impressive. I discovered later that this was for security reasons. Should a ruthless gang of terrorists get past Heinemann – and one good blast of his rotten breath should have been sufficient to immobilise them – and reach the Fifth Floor, the sheer size of the room would give time for a member of staff to press a warning buzzer and for the D-G to lock himself in a safe or self-destruct, depending upon his mood.

A green light flashed above his door, and I was invited to enter. Six men in dark suits sat facing me behind a polished conference table. Behind them on the wall were the portraits of the D-G's three predecessors, all, of course, heavily disguised. The six men were unrecognisable. Two of them had paper bags on their heads, the third a large HM Stationery Office envelope, the one in the middle a Popeye mask and the remaining two's faces were twisted into strange potato shapes by fish-net stockings.

Popeye spoke first. It was Charlie Orange. First he sounded welcoming, then he appeared apologetic.

'I'm afraid I can't understand a word you're saying' I said.

Popeye cursed indistinctly.

Charlie Orange removed his mask and winked.

'You knew who I was anyway, Barker – I never could do voices. Firstly I welcomed you on behalf of the Board, and apologised for their appearing incognito, but it makes life easier in the unlikely event that you fail. Now why do you want to join us?'

'You asked me' I replied.

'Good answer' said Charlie, and there was affirmative grunting from the Board. 'Now I think it should be made clear to you from the outset that the Security Service is nothing to do with the Civil Service. You won't get bumped up the Promotion ladder every few years as a matter of course. You're too old, for a start. So there's very little chance of your ever becoming a Senior Officer, virtually no chance of making Assistant Director, and absolutely no chance whatsoever of aspiring to one of the six Directorships, my word, no!' And he and the bags and the stockings began to shake with laughter. When at last he could control himself again he added, 'To be one of us, I am afraid, would require considerably more qualifications than you can muster.' He flicked through it briskly as if to confirm my dreadful lack of qualifications.

I told the Board frankly that, since I was by nature a lone furrower rather than one of life's bosses, this did not bother me at all.

'Funnily enough' said Charlie, 'those are to all intents and purposes exactly the same words that Peter Wright employed at his Board. Well, it didn't do him any harm. He got in all right, but we didn't make him any rash promises – the D-G here – '

he nodded to the Stationery Office envelope which I discovered later contained the head of Sir Dick Goldsmith White, 'told Wright he wasn't sure we needed an animal such as him in the Security Service – not an animal, of course, in that sense, but in the other, Wright being a technical wallah, and our not being – anyway the D-G said we'd give it a try if he would, and I think that would be our attitude to you.'

The various head-pieces nodded.

'I wonder, D-G' said Charlie, 'if you have anything to add?'

I had noticed that while Charlie had been speaking, the D-G had been enlarging his mouth-piece with the stem of his unlit pipe. Obviously, he had something to add.

'Jesmond, if I may call you that on such short acquaintance, though we tend here to use Christian names when addressing our juniors, who in their turn, let me stress, may call us "Sir", I'm going to start you off in A4. You'll be working with Gascoyne Balls, who I think you have met.'

I nodded. I was somewhat anxious, as the D-G while he spoke, was trying to light his pipe. He had already made four or five attempts, and I felt danger loomed.

'A4's the Watchers,' he said. 'Surveillance. Following Russians about. You think quickly, I gather. You may have some ideas. They seem to spot our fellows every time. Tell the truth, we're losing the Cold War rather badly.'

In his agitation, he attempted to light his pipe again, and set fire to his envelope. Luckily, under the window were three buckets of sand, and I was able to confirm my quick thinking by emptying one over his head. There was a ripple of applause from the Directorate.

'Thank you' White said, spitting sand into a drawer of his desk. 'I think we've made a very wise decision in your case. Good luck to you.'

After lunch, I made my way along the Fifth Floor for the routine interview with the Personnel Director, Harry Ladder.

'This is just a friendly chat' he said. 'Just to get to know you a bit.' He greeted me with a most peculiar hand-shake, his middle finger tickling my palm, then he rolled up his right trouser-leg and scratched his knee-cap ostentatiously. Seeing my puzzled expression, he laughed. 'Not of the Brotherhood, then? No matter. Though it does make life a bit easier.

All I've got to do is make sure you're not a Communist, which is bloody unlikely if your coming to work for MI5. We sent our tame Bluebottle round to the London Rubber Company and they said you hadn't been calling the Kremlin collect, or giving readings from *Das Kapital* in the Works Canteen, or learning the balalaika.' Suddenly he burst into song. 'Pom. Pom. Ti-pom-ti-pom-pom. Pom-ti-pom-pom-pom. What is that? I've been humming it all day.'

'We are the Ovaltinies?' I suggested. His rendition had not been particularly accurate.

'Were you ever one?' he asked quickly.

'Yes' I said.

'Good' he said. 'Boy Scout?'

'No' I said.

'Oh dear' he said. 'Ah well, no matter.' Ladder's desk was empty, so I imagined he had a tape-recorder somewhere. Perhaps that great Elk's head on the wall, the eyes seemed to follow me about. Then again, there was that great mirror on the wall. I fought an overpowering urge to write 'Piss off' on it backwards, and see if there was any reaction from behind it. It was the first of many occasions that I thought to myself that paranoia was never far away when one worked for the Secret Service.

'Voted Labour in 1945?'

I thought it might be best not to admit that I did, and pretended that I did not fully understand the question. I realised that this was a futile exercise when he took a folded ballot paper from his pocket, shook it open and revealed my large 'X' against the name of Herbert Morrison.

'Sorry' I said '*Nineteen*-forty-five? Ah yes. Yes, I did. Sorry.'

'Don't apologise' said Ladder. 'Almost everybody else did. Bit disillusioned now though, eh?'

'Deeply' I replied. 'I have no time whatsoever for the Labour Party. As to Communism, it is, in my view, evil and pernicious and I will do everything in my power to win the fight against it. No, I have been moving steadily right since 1945 –'

'Not too far, I hope' smiled Ladder.

'Oh no' I replied, first to the Elk, and then again to the mirror, just in case. 'Oh no. I abhor Fascism as keenly as I detest Communism.'

50

'Ever been queer?'

'What?' I blurted. The sudden change of tack had surprised me.

'Buggery?' he enquired. 'Are you interested in that sort of thing?'

'Not before lunch' I laughed nervously.

'Haven't you had lunch?' Ladder glanced at his watch.

'Yes, I have' I wasn't coming out of this any too well. 'I hate homosexuals. My brother, to whom I was very close, would beat them with a wet towel. I used to applaud loudly. Vile, vile people.'

Ladder walked around me slowly. He brushed some dandruff from my right shoulder. 'Well done' he said. 'Consider yourself vetted.' He shook my hand warmly. And that was all there was to it. Bloody hell, you're thinking, no wonder Burgess and Maclean and Philby and Blunt had minced so easily through the portals of Liberty Hall.

As I made for the door I was thinking of asking whether I had been surveyed by the Elk or the large mirror, when I noticed for the first time two open umbrellas on the floor in the corner. Ah, I muttered to myself, P. Wright rides again. Indeed, he was on a chair in the corridor outside, pretending to change a light-bulb. I wished him a Good Afternoon. He ignored me totally.

There was a training programme to be undergone before I officially joined MI5. This was run by an absolute bastard of an officer called Manslaughter. He was an aggressive, mean, humourless ogre who made the lives of young recruits fresh from the Universities a perfect hell. Admittedly they were not up to much, but his fuse was fearsomely short. He was always tearing their ears off or nailing their hands to the vaulting horse.

It came as no surprise to me when he resigned and went into the City. Practising what he had preached so ruthlessly to those trembling graduates, in no time at all he reached the top of the tree, yards ahead of the Fraud Squad. Nowadays, he is Lord Manslaughter and in charge of privatising almost everything from Water, Air, Earth and Fire to the Police. I must confess that he was always quite civil to me, perhaps because of my age. He would occasionally laugh at my deafness – he enjoyed and exploited weakness in others – but he gave me a sound grounding in the business of spying.

'You can do anything you bloody like, Barker, as long as it's for King and Country. Pillage and rape, if your whim so seizes you, you can rip up the Ten Commandments, one at a time, or altogether if you want, just don't break the Eleventh, eh? "Thou shalt not get nicked." Oh, the Met's OK, but if Special Branch ask you to come along noisily, so they can kick the shit out of you, then the Service tends to pretend that they have never previously laid eyes on you. That apart, you can have a wonderful time at the taxpayer's expense, matey!'

He taught us that MI5 was the best Intelligence Service in the world. The French were nothing but cissies, who simply played at it. The Americans were over-enthusiastic amateurs, who were given far too much money. He seemed to have more time for the KGB, whose interrogation techniques he particularly admired, ('They don't piss about, Barker') than he did for our colleagues in MI6. I was to discover that the two services were constantly at loggerheads.

A retired Special Branch policeman gave a series of lectures on a variety of subjects – How to Pick Locks with a Paper-Clip, How to Kill with a Sand-filled Sock, a Silk Tie or a Suit-case, How to Bring Down a Government with Simple Assassination or Blackmail Techniques, The Making of Poisons and Explosives from Everyday Household Accessories, and so on. All good, sensible stuff.

Manslaughter was taking the survivors of the course to date on an exercise in Snowdonia. The weather was appalling at that time of year. 'Been told to lose a few' he confided to me, laughing heartily. I was excused because of my years, but he left me a tape-recorder and a box full of large tape-reels. I watched from the window as Manslaughter threw hollow-eyed young men into the back of a Butcher's van, then turned and investigated the box. Manslaughter was clearly keen on Wagner and Vera Lynn. There printed on one spool I read, 'Sir Hugo Ruislip. After-Dinner Speech. Security Service Shindig. Savoy. Dec. 1950.' That, I thought, might well be worth listening to, Sir Hugo was something of a legend in the History of MI5. He had joined in the late 1920s when MI5 was in acute danger of being gobbled up by MI6. MI5 had got off to a lively start in 1909, at which time it was quite obvious that War loomed. The War Office realised that there needed to be some sort of organisation to flush out the large numbers of German spies who were flooding into the country. Anyone found wandering about in tweed suit, cricket pads and a spiked helmet, with an Anglo-German Phrase-book in hand, was seized and worked over, quite roughly, with a length of garden-hose. The only problem arose when the suspect was not wearing a spiked helmet and was related to Edward the Seventh. MI5 had a jolly good War. Alas, of course, in the post-war years there were fewer and fewer Germans to beat up, and little reason to, with the result that Government cut back MI5's resources severely. That was when MI6 made its bid for a take-over, and the day was saved by no less a person than Hugo Ruislip, who, after an excellent lunch at the Cavalry Club, came up with the Red Menace. This led to a tremendous revival of MI5 morale and activity, with the Famous Raid on the Soviet Trade Delegation in 1927, in which an enormously encouraging amount of evidence was discovered proving conclusively that Russia was up to no good at all, and MI5 was back in business. Ruislip and MI5 enjoyed a splendid World War II, and it was generally thought that he was the man to lead us into World War III and thereafter, if you believed in a thereafter. However that awful man Attlee, still irked after twenty years about MI5's attempt to bring down Ramsay Macdonald in 1923 with the Zinoviev Letter, put a boring old plod in charge of MI5 instead of Ruislip. Hugo, a thoroughly decent sort, tried to sweat it out under the New Management, but ran foul of the Burgess and Maclean business, broke down under the strain, went barking mad and was put in charge of Nuclear Weapon Testing.

I threaded the tape, a complicated business in those days, comparable in many ways to the camel and the needle's eye, and put on the heavy ear-phones. It was clear at once that Ruislip had had a few.

'The Service was formed to provide some sort of war-time occupation for men who would never fit into the military life and were too intelligent to be policemen. Intellectuals and writers like Somerset Maugham, Joseph Conrad, Ian Fleming, Compton Mackenzie, Graham Greene, Barbara Cartland, that sort of fellow. Well, that's all right, but come the peace it's another story, of course. Different kind of swots, entirely. Supercilious bastards in the main. And, to balance things up, Whoops! (There was a burst of mild laughter, and muffled grunting. Perhaps Sir Hugo had made some expansive gesture and fallen over.) Sorry about that. As you were. To balance things up, we'd got our swots, we hired some Old School Bullies. Fine, insensitive swine who could understand the thinking of the most bastardly of adversaries, because their dim minds had been trained to work in precisely the same way. Swots and Bullies. Swots and Bullies. That's the perfect combination for the Great Game. Men who could rise above thoughts of common decency, roar with laughter at notions of Fair Play, men who had happily lost their innocence, and more importantly, their guilt. Men who will roar with righteous indignation at the Club on hearing news of a Wild-cat Strike at a bicycle-factory in Hounslow, and then totter back to the Office to stick electrodes up some poor bastard's arse because his grandmother was Albanian. Oh, gentlemen, you are the strangest of bed-fellows. The Swots and the Bullies. (His delivery was now erratic. The drink did not help, but I think he was also unnerved by the steadily swelling rumble of disapproval from his audience.) Together you can wreak your vengeance on those who despised you at your Public Schools. You have the weapons, now, you have the techniques. You have the Faissez-Laire – Lucy Friar – Flossy – oh, bugger. You are a Grand and Holy Order of Shits, whose every sense is honed to the sharpness of the razor secreted in your bowler-hat. You live by the smell of fear, the taste of death, the sound of a widow screaming, the sight of a man broken on the wheel, the touch of the thumbscrew. All in the name of Kunt and Kingtry. Well now as Governor-General of the Bikini Atoll, I can atomise the fucking lot of you – !' (A band started playing and I could hear another voice encouraging the guests to dance. Sir Hugo became increasingly faint.) 'Boom! Boom! Bloody men!'

I switched off the tape-recorder and sat back in a chair with only three legs. Manslaughter's Number Two, Podmore, an ex-Petty Officer with a neck wider than his head, burst in. I had heard Manslaughter say that Podmore's War Record was one of the few you could dance to. He tore the tape of Hugo Ruislip from the machine and threw it into the box on the table. This he picked up, all in one easy movement, shouting, 'Wrong bloody box!', and hurling it into the empty grate, he then pulled a Verey pistol from his pocked and scored a direct hit on the box, which went up like a rocket.

'You didn't listen to any of that, did you?'

'No' I lied, 'I was thinking of listening to Vera Lynn – .'

'Oh, my God!' he cried. 'Was Dame Vera in there?' There was nothing to be done. There was a terrific blaze. In fact, I thought I could hear the bells of distant fire-engines.

'And Wagner' I said, adding to Podmore's misery. He staggered from the room, a shadow of his former self. I heard later that he shot himself with that self-same Verey pistol. There was a cover-up, of course, the suicide was written off as an accident, though it seemed to me to be an eccentric way to insert suppositories.

Only half the recruits came back from North Wales with Manslaughter, all a good deal sadder and, I imagine, none the wiser. However, he seemed in expansive mood, and suggested that he gave me a guided tour of the building. We marched down corridor after corridor, past door after door, each with some strange jumble of letters upon it, quite meaningless probably except to the occupants. These offices were all ridiculously over-crowded. Manslaughter threw open the odd door and heartily greeted those crushed inside. I could not help but notice that he never elicited a civil response. He was universally disliked. Only Peter Wright waved to him and smiled. He sat alone in a converted lavatory, crouched over equipment with his inevitable ear-phones on.

'Good bloke, Pete!' boomed Manslaughter. That is not what I had heard. Since his arrival he seemed to have done nothing but whinge about MI5's pathetically low technical know-how, his pay, the vetting process, and the fact that the Service spent the whole morning doing *The Times* crossword. (At least, my appointment might speed up that process. I think that's why I was taken on.) Anyway, the Directorate saw a future for him, and his bugging research was going ahead apace. How fortunate, I thought, as I wondered what they had in mind for me, that our paths were unlikely to cross again. Little did I know.

My last day of training was a tour of the Registry. This is the massive filing system that covers the entire ground-floor of Leconfield House. There's probably a file on you there somewhere, gentle reader, I don't see why not, everybody else is in there.

Roger HOLLIS & Predecessors.

6

They really didn't know what to do with me. For a time I worked with the Post Office Special Investigations Unit at their HQ near St Pauls'. MI5 had offices and laboratories there. Our man in charge at the time was one Colonel Treadmill, who relished his work. There were Special Investigations Unit Rooms all over the country, constantly probing letters and parcels and tapping telephones. I was amazed at the size of the task. There were over twenty Post Office chaps alone at our main office, ferreting away at the Royal Mail. You could hardly see them sometimes for the steam from their kettles. If that apparently primitive system didn't work they would hold the envelope up to a bright light, or if that failed, fall back on the old split-bamboo techniques, which dates back to Ancient China, who were as nosey as us. The only way to frustrate the lads, and it still works today, is to sellotape both ends of the envelope. Then major decisions had to be reached involving the Deputy Director-General of MI5 – whether or not to tear open the letter or parcel, and then either lose it altogether or send it on, covered in apologies from the Post Office for careless handling. The contents of all this mail was micro-filmed and sent off to the great filing cabinets at the Registry.

It explained a lot to me about the postal services in Britain. No small wonder that the only mail that seems to get through on time, and undamaged, are those nasty brown envelopes with little windows that arrive On Her Majesty's Service. It also explains why the Post Office will never be privatised. Try and explain all that away in the brochure.

I will confess to quite enjoying the laboratories. Chemists, surrounded by bubbling test tubes and retorts, experimenting with invisible ink and other tricks of the secret trade. How well I remember holding a piece of blank paper over a bunsen-burner and watching with fascination as large, clear letters emerged.

'ROTT OFF, MIZERUBLE MI5 SNOOPIE. HOPES YOUR BALLOX FELL OFF. MARY KRISTMUS, BUS-TARD. HO. HO. HO.'

The other laboratories where MI5 and the Post Office capered hand-in-hand were at Dollis Hill. Here they were applying new and sophisticated processes to phone-tapping, slowly revolutionising the system, and cutting down on the mass of wires and leads and umbrellas that usually led quite quickly to the discovery of an operation. There was a good deal they were learning to do by remote control, which meant we no longer had to infiltrate Embassies and stick microphones in their telephones. We seemed to have most Russian diplomats covered, and the resultant tapes and acetates were sent up to the seventh floor at HQ which was full of Tzarist Russians, full-bearded old aristocrats, all quite mad and mostly as deaf as myself.

There had been talk of my helping out with the Watchers, and I was quite relieved when I was transferred to them and no longer required to foul up the Postal Services. It was immediately apparent where their problems lay. I was given an address in Kensington Park Gardens, directly opposite the Russian Embassy. There on the first floor was a full Surveillance Unit, packed into a smoke-filled room, bored, tired and thoroughly demoralised. Equipment was everywhere and piles of files lay scattered on the floor. Every time a diplomat appeared through the gate, a photographer would photograph him, an agent with a telescope would name him and shout a number, and a wireless operator would relay the number to a waiting car. In the car were the traditional team of three Watchers – one on the radio, one with the London A–Z, and one driver. I couldn't help noticing that several of the diplomats waved to our window. I was up there for several days checking recent photographs of diplomats against those in the files, usually out-of-date passport photographs, bearing little similarity to the man today.

At the start of my second week, I travelled in one of the pursuit vehicles as map-reader. Once again it seemed a useless occupation. Three times on that first Monday we set off after three different diplomats, each, within the first mile, turned to us, raised his hat, and lost us. The third time, in our desperation, we hit a bus. The Watchers definitely had problems, and damned if I could think of an answer.

I was saved from having to offer one by 'Buster' Crabbe, the doomed frog-man. This monster cock-up by MI6 caused a reshuffle at the top and our D-G. Dick White left, with some reluctance, to sort out that branch of the Service. They definitely needed help. Fancy sending a man of Crabbe's age and condition out in snorkel and flippers to probe round the back of a Russki battleship. In a *British* port. With Krushev and Bulganin aboard, no less. I ask you.

The new D-G was Roger Hollis who had been Whites' Number Two. I was absolutely astonished to receive a summons to his office. He was lying on the floor, sighing deeply, surrounded by files. He looked utterly exhausted. He gestured to me to lie down beside him.

'We've got a problem, Barker. Well, *I* have a problem and I'd like to share it with you. You have a fresh, keen eye and you're not doing anything useful at the moment. I may have made a terrible mistake. I've received a letter from J. Edgar Hoover. The FBI have been running a cipher check in the Czech Embassy in Washington. Now this chap, Frantisek Tisler, went home on holiday, met up with and got roaring pissed with an old chum of his, the Czech Military Attaché in London, one Colonel Pribyl, who, in his cups revealed that the Russkis have got a spy in MI5, and he could prove it. Apparently he was driving one of his more important agents around London, de-briefing him on somesuch, when he realised that he was being followed by the Watchers – three blokes in a car, and the number plates revolving like a fruit machine (not too hard to spot), and he made a point of losing them – none too difficult. Now Pribyl had to make damned certain that the Watchers hadn't got a "make" I believe the Americans call it, on his agent, so he rang up his opposite number at the Russian Embassy, who said "Give me a couple of days and I'll check it out" or words to that effect. Back he comes, two days later, no panic, the Watchers had no idea who he was, and had been giving each other driving lessons. Anyway, adds the Russki, the Watchers aren't following diplomats from outside their Embassies any more, new system at work, they're picking them now on the bridges as they cross the Thames. This apparently makes it a bloody sight harder for the Russkis to monitor our chaps.'

'Why?' I said. God, this floor was playing havoc with my back.

'How should I know?' snapped Hollis. 'That is what the Technical Johnnies tell me.'

I nodded. That was good enough for me. I have found that not only can you blind me with science, you can also give me severe migraines with it, and a sense of total inadequacy.

'Is it true that the Watchers have changed their system?' That would seem to prove that there was a double-agent at work in Leconfield House.

'It is true' said Hollis, 'and I have a pretty good idea who it is.' He handed me a large blue file. 'Thumb through this and tell me what you think.' It was an extraordinary tale that was unveiled of five years of bugging and burglary across London at the State's behest. There seemed to be no place in the Great Metropolis left unbugged. And while it seemed reasonable to comprehensively bug the Headquarters of the British Communist Party it was scarcely hospitable to bug every room in Lancaster House, home of the Colonial Conference and such. It was, however, in operations against the Russians that a pattern began to emerge.

Disguised as decorators, MI5 had entered a house next door to the Russian Consulate in the Bayswater Road and put a probe microphone in the communicating wall. Six months later, it went dead. MI5 had an agent working as an odd-job man for the Russians and he reported that the room had been redecorated. Even so, as the microphone pinhole was some fourteen feet up and hidden by some elaborate plaster-work, it seemed unlikely that it had been painted over – an inch of plaster had been injected down the pinhole with a hyperdermic syringe.

Hollis asked me what I was laughing at, and when I explained, he said it could well have been pure luck that the pin-hole had been discovered. It seemed reasonable that the Russians would study Party walls fairly carefully. At the same time all bugs placed are logged, with their precise location, and recorded in an Index. He tapped the side of his nose.

There was a catalogue of similar coincidences in Canada and Australia. In Canada a wall stiff with microphones and cables, and virtually indetectable, was built by the Mounties in an old building the Poles were having renovated as a Consulate. Within two weeks, the Poles had had it knocked down and another erected. In Canberra, listening devices were installed in the window frames of the KGB resident's room. They heard him whistle, sing, curse and fart. But the man never spoke.

Operation MOLE, Operation CHOIR, Operation DEW-WORM, all hailed on their instigation as technical triumphs, were all absolute flops as far as Intelligence was concerned.

'It all points to there being an Enemy Within,' said Hollis. I could hear the capital letters. 'Someone has blabbed.'

'Could that someone be whoever it was that put the bugs in in the first place?' I asked. 'Thus cutting out the middle man.'

My theory precisely' replied Hollis, 'and that is why, as I said, I think I have made a great mistake.'

'Who then is the bugging burglar and vice versa?' I enquired.

'The very man whom I have asked to look into this Watchers business.' said Hollis, leaping to his feet and heading for the drinks cabinet. 'And the man I want to pursue to the ends of the Earth.' He poured himself a large one. 'Peter bloody Wright.'

I'd thought so all the time, but I hadn't said a word as the one thing I had learned in my brief association with the Secret Service is that the Heads of it do enjoy their moments of high drama. I only wished I could have provided dramatic chords play-ed by the London Philharmonic to punctuate his utterances.

'He's not one of us, Jesmond. He resents us. He could be one of them. Check him out. Ask around. Mrs Beardmore's good. Talk to her. She knows everything that goes on here.'

'Right, Sir' I said. He seemed to have forgotten that I wasn't one of him either. 'Where do I find Mrs Beardmore?'

'Behind her tea-trolley, Barker, wherever that may be.'

Mrs. Deirdre Beardmore, M.B.E.

7

Now I've got to plod the mean streets endlessly like George Smiley or is it Alec Guinness? I don't look like either of them. I've also got to find time to read through every one of something akin to 270 million files at the Registry. Spying is a lonely business. But first, I plod the mean corridors of Leconfield House in search of Mrs Beardmore and her trolley. I imagined when Hollis had first mentioned her that she would be one of those pleasingly eccentric old dears who had given 40 years to the Service, and retired to gin and gentle gardening, would know everyone and be played by Miss Beryl Reid. I found her on the fourth floor, played by Joan Crawford. Well, fatter perhaps but I would imagine an equally dab hand with a coat-hanger. I showed her my identification and helped her push her trolley into an empty office. I mentioned Roger Hollis's name and she beamed contentedly.

''is father was the Bishop of Taunton' she proclaimed.

'I really want to talk about Peter Wright' I said, watching her beam go out.

''e dislikes Roger intensely. I've 'eard 'im say so in the Canteen. 'e's always moaning about something. Lumps in the custard, or a rubber glove in 'is steak and kidney pudding, or the appalling state of the relationship with the FBI.'

Suddenly a thought struck me and I realised that I was laughably naïve and inexperienced to be undertaking this job for Hollis. I turned Mrs Beardmore's tea-urn on full-blast, and under cover of the noise of her thick brew splashing on the linoleum, I whispered:

'Are we secure, Mrs Beardmore?'

Here I was, against the master-bugger and it had never even occurred to me to check out Hollis's office. I imagined that Wright had peppered the walls, light-fittings, filing cabinets, and floor of Hollis's office with listening devices. Even now Wright was probably playing back the acetate of our conversation about him, and shaking with silent laughter. No, that was Mrs Beardmore. She appeared to be in the grips of a terminal fit of the giggles. She rolled in the lukewarm tea, clutching her ample sides.

'Ho deary, deary me.' she gurgled finally, wiping her eyes with her grubby apron 'That was funny. 'e bugged a fairy-cake, and I ate it!'

'How do you know?' I hissed.

'The wire was still attached, so I pulled it out again. It was a glacé cherry. I was violently sick in the chutney.' And she began to hoot again. I was crawling around the tiny office searching for some sort of microphone, some tell-tale wires.

'It's all right, Mr Barker,' said Mrs Beardmore weakly, ''e 'asn't bugged the second floor yet.' I helped her up. The room was awash. I sat her down.

'Mrs Beardmore' I said, 'have you heard Mr Wright speak recently about the Watchers, in particular the fact that the Russians seem to know their every movement before they make it, their special peculiarities, their hobbies and their hat-sizes?'

'Only yesterday' replied Mrs Beardmore, ''e was bumbling away to himself in the Self-service Cafeteria. 'e was writing things down on a paper doily, and bumbling about an Operation RAFTER. 'e's always bumbling about an Operation something. Operation this, Operation that. Here's the doily.' I would de-cypher it later. 'Mrs Beardmore, you should have been a spy.'

'I was once approached by the KGB in Tesco's' said Mrs Beardmore proudly, 'but I told them where they could stuff their wire basket full of roubles.'

'Keep your eyes and ears open, Mrs Beardmore, and report

to me daily. There could be an MBE in this for you.'

With one movement, her hands leapt to the neck of her soggy overall and she tore it open. My God, was this the prelude to sex or violence? Neither, we are not in 007 country. There, hanging between her tremendous, liver-spotted breasts, hung the insignia of a Member of the British Empire. I smiled.

'I see your loyalty has already been rewarded.'

She put a finger to her lips. ''ush-'ush' she whispered. 'I must get out of these nasty wet things.'

I hurried off quickly to the lift before I fell victim to Lust's saucy proddings. I am not made of stone, and this is not that sort of book.

Roger Hollis was in his office when I entered unannounced. Before he could speak, I had clapped a hand over his mouth. With the other hand, I scrawled on his blotter, 'YOUR OFFICE IS PROBABLY BUGGED.' And to give the message added weight, I signed it. Hollis pulled my hand away from his mouth and spat a good deal of beef and bread into his waste-paper basket. I hadn't realised that he had been in the middle of his lunch.

'ST JAMES' PARK' he wrote on the blotter. 'FOLLOW ME.' Then he fed the blotter into his shredder. We tip-toed from his office.

We had also fed his sandwiches through the shredder and both carried burn-bags full of breadcrumbs for the ducks and pelicans. Hollis shooed a pelican away and spoke.

'Wright came to see me this morning' said Hollis, 'to report on this Watchers' business. He's cracked it.'

'He's confessed!' I cried. He had listened in to Hollis and me and the knowledge that we were on to him had proved too much. Perhaps I'd get the MBE

'No he hasn't!' snapped Hollis. 'It was the Russians all the time. The bastards have been monitoring Watcher communications for years. It explains everything quite satisfactorily. Nobody in MI5 leaked anything, they were listening to our chaps on the radio all the time. But, and it's a big but – ' So big that it caused a flock of pigeons to rise in panic and flap way over the Foreign Office. 'Wright has come up with RAFTER. Bloody clever. Now we can monitor them, and know precisely when they are monitoring us. The bloody Yanks haven't got anything like that. We've jumped ahead of them technically, Barker. Now I've instructed Wright to go over to America and rub Hoover's nose in it. Ha! Ha! Ha!' In his joy he lashed out at a goose with his umbrella.

'You haven't' I said quickly, 'read this paper doily. It speaks of a "two-legged source".'

'Probably his shopping list,' said Hollis airily. 'Something new from Cross and Blackwell.'

I spelt 'source' for him. 'This doily definitely suggests that, although the Russians were hanging onto our every word for years, there is still enough evidence to suggest the presence of a mole in MI5.'

Hollis now held his umbrella like a shot-gun and was blazing away at any fowl that moved.

'Is it likely, Barker, I ask you, that if Wright *were* working for the KGB he would suggest on a doily that someone in MI5 *was* working for the KGB, when he has just submitted a report to me that, in his view, no-one is working for the KGB?'

'Did he deliberately leave that doily in the Cafeteria knowing that Mrs Beardmore, MBE, would in all probability, pass it on to someone higher up?'

'A double-bluff?' Hollis had stopped alarming birds, and was looking at one with renewed respect. 'Barker, Jesmond, even, you are beginning to think like a spy. That is very good.'

'It says here' I waved the doily, 'and I quote, "Where *was* Pribyl?" Unquote.'

'Ah,' said Hollis, 'Pribyl was going to meet one of his agents on the South Downs as per usual. We decided Special Branch should avert them both. This agent, chap called Linney, was working on guided missiles for the RAF. Tisler told us that, the Czech chappie. Well, Linney turned up. Pribyl didn't. Who warned Pribyl?'

'Wright' I said.

'And again,' added Hollis, 'was he warned? Perhaps he decided not to go. Perhaps he forgot to go. One must never overlook the simple, straightforward answer. Czechs aren't like us, you know. They're not sticklers for punctuality. He may have gypsy blood. Who knows?'

'That's not all' I said, 'There's – '

'Don't' rapped Hollis, 'confuse me with details! That's your department. I am responsible for the broad view. Policy, that sort of thing. I'm bloody hungry, incidentally. No lunch, that's it. I'm off to the Club. You keep your eye on him, then, but I think you're wasting your time. I like him, and I'm certain he's very fond of me . . .'

Oh dear, I thought, and then, ah, well, orders are orders. Keep an eye on him, Hollis had said, I will go and see Ambler in Transport about an aeroplane to Washington.

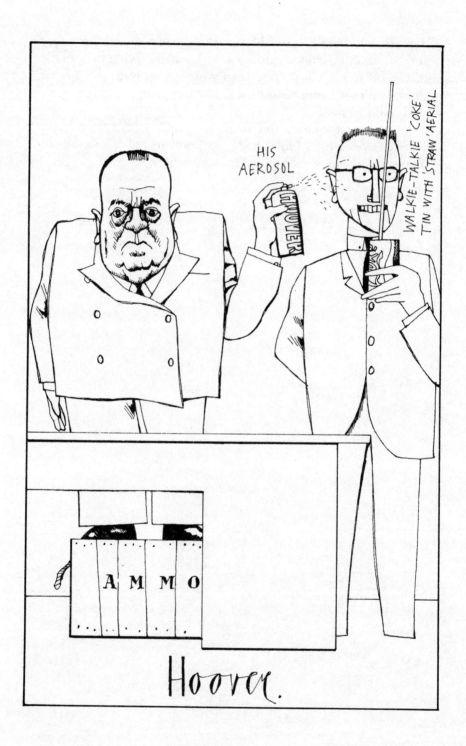

Hoover.

8

So there I was in Washington in springtime, and very lovely it was too. The thinnest of drizzles, but I didn't know a single soul. After Hollis came back from lunch, I told him I was leaving for America but I don't think he heard me. There was probably, almost certainly an MI5 Office in Washington, but I had no idea where, and it was unlikely to be in the Yellow Pages. The FBI offices were easy enough to find – they do tours – but I doubted if they would include a trip around Hoover's office, and if they did, it would be stretching good fortune too far if Wright was there at the time doing his bit for MI5.

My brief period with the Watchers served me in good stead. I positioned myself at the entrance of the Bureau, and looked up at the building opposite. It was some sort of office building, and there on the fourth floor were two windows with curtains. I walked across the road, entered the building and ascended to the fourth floor. I kept an eye on the corridor. The office I was most certain of had a notice on the door announcing that it was closed for renovations. My suspicions were confirmed when a tall man in braces came out of it, to return ten minutes later with cartons of hamburgers and coffee. I waited a few minutes, then knocked on the door. The occupants were naturally reluctant to answer, but, finally a head peered at me round the door.

'Peter in?' I enquired blithely, raising my hat.

'What?' They never are too bright – the Watchers.

'Peter Wright' I said, flashing my identity.

'Oh, come on in' the tall man waved me welcome. 'Friend of Peter's' he called out to the others. In the main office were all the traditional trappings of surveillance – telescope, cameras, tape-recorders, the rotting remains of fast food, empty polystyrene mugs and overflowing ashtrays. There were three of them, they introduced themselves, but I wasn't listening. I always think of them as Freeman, Hardy and Willis.

'Peter Wright strikes again, eh?' I laughed.

'Well,' said Freeman, 'it's second nature to him isn't it? He goes somewhere, he bugs it. Force of habit. And Mr. Hoover's office, well, I suppose that was what the Missing Link would be to David Attenborough.'

'He should be in in a minute' said Hardy, handing me a pair of earphones. 'He's a card, isn't he?'

'He's an asshole' said Willis. Opinions always seemed sharply divided about Wright. The general view appeared to be that he was extremely full of himself, firmly convinced that he was God's gift to MI5.

'He's going in now' said Hardy. I put on my earphones.

The interview between Hoover and Wright was largely a one-sided affair. As instructed by Hollis, Wright did all he could to keep to the technical side of the Pribyl Affair. Hoover, on the other hand, was determined to point out the appalling slackness of MI5 in tackling the Russian threat, and when he got on to the subject of Burgess and Maclean Willis turned the volume down. Hoover then pointed out that that sort of thing could never happen at the Bureau, where he personally vetted every officer. I almost felt sorry for Peter Wright as he was put through the mangle. I wondered idly if this tape would ever be heard in London.

Suddenly, it was over. Wright was saying, 'Thank you Mr Hoover. Thank you very much, Sir. Thank you.' His voice growing fainter as he reversed out of the door. He had been instructed to grovel. Hoover liked it.

'I think he put the bug under his chair' said Hardy.

All you could hear now through the ear-phones were gales of laughter. At last, Hoover's voice cut through –

'OK that's enough, men! I want new wall-paper, curtains

and carpet now! That Limey looked sickly.'

The room emptied and then came the sound of decorators. I thought I might leave before Wright came up – after all, I had not been invited.

'He's seeing James Angleton of the CIA tomorrow' said Freeman.

'I know' I lied.

★   ★   ★

Two hours later, I was ushered in to Hoover's freshly decorated office. I have never been in a place so aggressively clean as the Headquarters of the FBI (well, you wouldn't in England, and apart from my visit to Dunkirk, I'd never previously been abroad). White tiles gleamed everywhere even in their mouths. Everywhere were clean young agents with sparkling, perfect teeth, impeccable suits and neat, clean hair. The place was spotless. Polished, burnished, scrubbed, dusted, Hoovered in fact. The man was obviously mad. He stood on a box behind his desk. There was a minion with bulging armpits at either side of him. Hoover looked like a dead dog.

'You say you have important news from Mr Roger Hollis.' His voice was a menacing hiss.

'May I sit?' I enquired. I was quite looking forward to the next bit. I sat down and immediately plucked Wright's tiny bug from under the chair. 'I thought this might interest you.' I threw it on to Hoover's desk. A minion picked it up and showed it to Hoover, who grunted, and handed it back to the minion, who popped it between his perfect teeth and bit it to death. Lord knows the effect on Hardy's ears across the road.

'Mr Wright, I presume?' said Hoover.

'Yes,' I replied. 'Sorry about that. He has his funny little ways.'

'Very decent of you, Mr Barker' said Hoover. 'Obviously you are a man we can trust.' He signalled his minions to squirt air-freshener in my direction. 'This Wright, is he clean?'

'I've never looked,' I said.

'I mean, is he to be trusted?'

'We harbour grave doubts.'

'And you would like me to place the services of the Bureau at your disposal. To check out our sources.'

'Would be grateful, Sir.'

Hoover began to flick a feather-duster at me. I don't think he realised that he was doing this. I put it down to a nervous tic. The man was barking mad.

'Why haven't you nailed Philby?' snapped Hoover suddenly.

'Philby?' I asked. 'MI6 cleared him, didn't they?' Harold Macmillan himself rose in the House and pronounced him pure as the driven.'

'Philby is a Bolshevik' pronounced Hoover. 'So for that matter is Harold Macmillan in all probability. Your whole country is riddled with them. The price of liberty, Mr Barker, is Eternal Violence. Rise up, and smite the ungodly.'

I was half-way out of my chair before I realised that he was waxing biblical. Perhaps we needed a bit of that at Leconfield House.

'Were I to tell you, Mr Barker, that not only is there a third man, Philby, but a fourth! And, indeed a fifth! What would you say to that Mr Barker?'

'Oh, Shit' I said.

'Wash out your mouth, Mr Barker! Fetch gargle!' he shouted to a minion. 'I will not have foul language employed within the walls of my Bureau. Were you one of my agents you would be stripped of your gun, your badge, your pension, your home, your wife and your family! Consider yourself fortunate, Mr Barker, that you are not in my employ.'

I thought he was going to fall off his box. I imagined the decorators would be back in action, minutes after I left. I'd learned something and I'd scattered a little seed upon the ground so I left. I was nearly through the door when Hoover shouted, 'You haven't said Thank you, Mr Hoover, thank you very much!'

'Thank you, Mr Hoover, thank you very much,' I said, and ran for my life past the shining tiles.

As I hurried down the front steps of the Bureau a burly man in a snap-brimmed hat asked me the time, and that was the last thing I remembered.

Whatever it was they shot up me must have been good stuff, as I awoke from it feeling better than I had for some time.

'Where am I?' I enquired brightly.

'OK Wright, spill it' said a voice. There was a bright light shining in my eyes, but, really, I didn't mind at all.

'Or the priest gets it?' I asked. I've studied their culture.

'You know who we are?' What ugly voices. Harsh and flat.

'FBI?' I suggested.

'Nope'

'CIA then' I said. How nice.

'Why did you see Hoover?'

'What a charmer' I smiled happily. 'What a gay old dog.'

'You'd know all about that, Wright. The whole of MI5's fucking queer.'

'Not guilty old fruit.' Nothing was going to upset my cheerful state. 'I've had enough trouble round the front of my fellow man. Not even my brother Fenton, an animal in matters sexual, stooped, if that's the word, to that sort of thing.'

'Goddam faggots!' There seemed to be about three of them. Their methods seemed rather basic. Where was Mr Nice Guy?

'Get this, Wright, you lousy motherfucker – ' Ah, here he is, I thought. Hello, Mr Nice Guy. 'You ain't gonna get nothin' outa Hoover.'

'One moment' I said. 'Before we go any further and you begin to lop off your lengths of rubber-hose, I am not Peter Wright.'

'Ah, shit!' said Mr Nice Guy.

'You wouldn't say that to J. Edgar' I cooed. The three of them moved off into a corner for a whispered conference. It sounded agitated. One of them came over to me.

'Who the hell are you, then?'

'Jesmond Barker, MI5' I lied. Or I was fairly convinced that I lied. I don't know what they'd given me but, by Gadfrey, I'd like the address of their chemist. He went back to the corner. Further whispering, then they all came back.

'What did Wright give Hoover? He must have given him some dam' thing. MI5's lickin' ass, ain't it? Hollis was when he came over. He was all over Hoover like a Puerto Rican massoose; and didn't Hoover love that. Nothin' that old asshole likes more than an English gentleman grovelling at his feet. So what did Wright give Hoover?'

'RAFTER' I said. I was determined to play hard to get. My lips were sealed.

'What's RAFTER?'

'I don't know' I said, 'but everyone's jolly pleased with it.'

'You'll find, Barker, that we ain't ungenerous where our friends are concerned. Can you get us the details on this RAFTER?'

'Oh yes' I lied, cheerfully and successfully. The drug was wearing off.

'OK. Get him back to his hotel. Put a bag over his head.'

'Could I,' I asked, 'have another shot of whatever? That was delicious.'

'OK Jesmond.'

'Whoopee!' I said.

9

After the excitement of Washington, I very nearly died of boredom back in London. Trailing Peter Wright became a snoring, boring chore. Mrs Beardmore told me he was in a state of high excitement about RAFTER. He really felt that he was dragging MI5 single-handed into the Age of Technology. To be fair, I quite enjoyed watching him apply his RAFTER to the Russian Embassy. I used to watch from a deck-chair in Kensington Gardens, that old hunting ground, and occasionally, I doffed my hat in memory of those martyred dwarfs. MI5 bought a house in the middle of the Russian diplomatic complex and installed one of the Bertram Mills Circus family. It was good fun to watch clowns, aerialists and jugglers tumble out of the back of a garish lorry carrying boxes and tubs full of MI5 equipment, and erecting high-wires and trapezes in the back garden. It was brilliant cover, quite unobtrusive, and would not appear at all odd to the Russians, who, doubtless, had installed the State Circus in close proximity to the British Embassy in Moscow. But after that it became deadly dull.

For month after month I trailed Wright's van around Battersea, Clapham and Wandsworth, with not the faintest idea of what he was doing. The nights I wasted parked on bomb-sites, up side-streets, in pub car-parks. It was invariably drizzling. If, as I imagined, he was trying to pinpoint some agent, receiving wireless messages from Moscow and responding, bloody RAFTER would seem to be something of a failure. At one stage he even transferred all his gubbins on to an RAF transport plane and flew backwards and forwards over London. This led to the entire operation moving north to Finsbury Park, where nothing happened either. Then he gave all that up as a bad job and moved into the Hyde Park Hotel. At least it was warm in the lobby. I would sit there, behind *The Times* crossword, watching cabin-trunks and laundry-baskets vanishing upstairs. I presumed that Wright's budget was somewhat over-stretched as he was still using the same Circus van, clowns and trapeze artists to shift his equipment. I thought the Hyde Park Hotel showed enormous tolerance.

It slowly dawned upon me, as I sat there, exactly what Wright was up to. The Hyde Park Hotel is but a *boule*-toss from the French Embassy. At the time, for reasons I could never understand, Harold Macmillan was desperately trying to get Britain into the Common Market. It would excite the Foreign Office no end to know what General de Gaulle's views were. The fact that no-one was in any doubt as to the General's views, which could best be summarised in the single word '*Non!*', was irrelevant. The Operation, code-named STOCKADE, was declared a triumph. Our lads, with the help once again of the Post Office, had entered the French Embassy, laid their bugs, and gained access to every cable from de Gaulle to the French Ambassador and vice versa. Another bloody nose for Froggy! De Gaulle still said '*Non!*' Ah, well.

★   ★   ★

I had not seen Hollis for some time, having nothing to report of any import. I arranged to meet him one afternoon in St James' Park. He arrived on the bridge slightly late and the worse for lunch.

'Bloody Wright' he said.

I nodded so vigorously in agreement that my bowler-hat fell in the lake. I wrote it off to experience.

'Bloody Wright' repeated Hollis. My toupee was now at risk. 'He's kite-flying again.'

'That's my department!' I shouted angrily. Admittedly, the department had been closed for years.

'No, no,' said Hollis impatiently, 'not *that* bloody nonsense.

Another bloody nonsense. Penetration at a relatively high level. That's what he's mooting again. I told him if we put the beaters in, it'll have an appalling effect on morale.'

'What set him off this time?' I asked.

'It's the Watchers again,' said Hollis.

'But the Russians have always known what they're doing!' I replied.

'Well, this time, the Watchers all went up to the Midlands on some wild-goose chase, so there was no surveillance on Russian diplomats. Wright thought it would be clever to keep Watcher HQ transmitting as per normal, so the Russkis would think we were still following them. Thirty-six hours after the lads headed up the M1, the Russian monitor is closed down.'

'They'd realised they weren't being followed. If you think about it, it took them quite a long time to look in the rear-view mirror.'

'Perhaps' sighed Hollis. He was not a happy man. 'Anyway, six weeks later, the Watchers return, resume surveillance, and half-an-hour later the Russian monitor is on again. That, in Peter Wright's view, is sufficient evidence to set up an Inquiry.'

'Is it reasonable to enquire who set up the Red Herring in the Midlands? Who sent all the Watchers in London after it? What –?'

'I told him to Piss Off,' said Hollis.

'Oh, yes' said Hollis, 'carry on with that. We haven't heard the last of this bloody business. Oh, my word, no.'

★   ★   ★

Then came the Lonsdale Case which was later described as 'a personal triumph for Peter Wright'. For myself, it was a personal disaster. Mrs Beardmore informed me over a slice of delicious fruitcake that a Polish Intelligence Officer, eager to defect, (known to MI5 as LAVINIA – God, some of our code-names are so stupid) had revealed that the Russians had two very important spies in Britain – one in British Intelligence and the other in the Navy. This was confirmed by Pincher, the lavatory attendant in the basement – a reliable source. Well, if P. Wright, Esquire, was the one in British Intelligence, then he would soon be making a move. I must be on my toes. I was. From the start I could see that he was directing all his attention on the Navy spy. Well, in the immortal words of Mandy Rice-Davies, he would, wouldn't he? This was a man named Houghton from the Underwater Weapons Establishment down in Dorset. As a matter of form I checked him out in the Registry and there he was. His wife had suggested he was a spy some years previously after he had left her for some sauce-box who worked underwater with him. He was apparently constantly meeting with sinister-looking foreigners, and had a good deal of money tucked away in his potting shed. The accusations had been ignored – Hell having no fury like a woman, etc. Ah, well.

Anyway, Pincher told me in hushed tones under the door, crouched on the cold tiles, as I engaged in a rip-roaring evacuation, that 'our lot' were back onto Houghton, and had found out his contact, a larger fish altogether, one Gordon Lonsdale, who Houghton and his fancy-woman Ethel came up to London to meet monthly. Lonsdale had been bugged in a big way – his appartment near Regent's Park, and his Wardour Street office. Our Gordon was something of a rakehell. Wright & Co were busy as bees. While Lonsdale had been in America, they had removed a suitcase and parcel from his safety deposit box at the Midland Bank and found a treasure-trove – a Complete Spy Kit, a Minox camera, code-books, maps and cigarette-lighters that weren't cigarette-lighters at all. No wonder they were excited. They took the suitcase out of the bank twice, and then discovered that the Russians had been monitoring them on both occasions despite the lateness of the hour. This had Wright shouting 'Leak!' again and 'High-level penetration!' and had me back in Hollis' office once again.

I explained my theory about Wright's behaviour and Hollis quite liked it. 'Soon,' I said, 'he's got to do something about Lavinia's other revelation, if he's our man.'

'If Lonsdale doesn't come back from his trip' said Hollis, 'then the Russians know for sure that we're on to him, and it will be proof positive that someone on one of our upper floors is blabbing.'

Lonsdale came back next day, and Wright suddenly started making trips by night to Ruislip, an address in Cranleigh Gardens. I used to watch with fascination as he left his car some distance from the house, and then approached it with the stealth of a cat-burglar. It was time for me to take the offensive. I went down to the stores and withdrew a telescope, a camera, a thermos flask and a rifle – a Lee-Enfield 303 – the only weapon I had ever half-mastered. All this was cleverly disguised by the Quartermaster as fishing-tackle, and thus armed I set off for Cranleigh Gardens, Ruislip. I moved in to the house opposite Wright's bolt-hole. As luck would have it, a room on the first floor facing the road was available! The occupants were a charming pair of booksellers (a saintly trade), from New Zealand, named Kroger. Peter and Helen, as I came to know them, could not have been more hospitable. There was another paying-guest, but I never met him, he came in late at night and was gone before breakfast. I settled in for a long watch. There was considerable activity in the house opposite. I noted every movement in my log. Wright only appeared occasionally, but other decidedly Slavonic-looking people were forever to-ing and fro-ing. I was not going to say a word to Hollis until I was certain. I lay low, but I kept one up the spout.

As I said, the Krogers made delightful hosts. I remember coming upon them one evening engaged in a lively discussion conducted in a language that was unknown to me. I asked them what language it was, and they told me that it was Maori. They seemed to have a wide range of interests.* Peter, I discovered, was something of a radio 'ham'. He spent hours tinkering with an elaborate wireless set. He tried to explain in layman's terms some of its workings, but I am a poor listener when matters technical are raised.

'You should meet Peter Wright.' I laughingly suggested to him.

'Who is Peter Wright?' asked Kroger.

'Oh, a chap at work, an absolute wiz at that sort of thing.' I nodded towards his impedimenta.

'What is your work?' asked Helen Kroger, and there, I must admit, she had me. Everything had happened so quickly that I had clean forgotten to provide myself with any sort of 'cover'.

---

*Helen Kroger had an interesting hobby for a woman. She was forever poring over books and magazines about American Military Aircraft. She was most knowledgeable. What a joyous surprise it must have been for her when she discovered that Ruislip was so close to a number of American Air Force installations!

'I am, in fact, retired now' I said slowly, playing for time, 'but when I worked, which I did for all my working life, I worked as a –' and I embarked on a simulated coughing-fit that would have made La Dame aux Camel Filters green with envy. Helen fetched me a glass of water, and while my mind raced, I made a lengthy business of recovery.

'I was in the Meteorological Office' I said, hawking and choking. When in doubt, fall back on the truth. (*Handy tips for Agents in the Field* – an MI5 handbook, p. 715). The cough I said was a legacy from too many hours on the roof in heavy drizzle. I was saved from further embroidery by the bell. The telephone rang. Peter answered it, said 'hello' several times and then replaced the receiver slowly. He and Helen exchanged an anxious glance. Helen seized me and began to push me upstairs, saying that in the wake of such an attack, the best thing I could do would be to lie down. I agreed with her, and put up no resistance. My last sight of Peter was darting about their living room, picking up Helen's books and magazines and throwing them on the fire.

As I lay on my bed, somewhat puzzled I must confess, I could hear the Krogers rushing about the house. The lavatories were flushed with amazing regularity. They were shouting to each other in Maori. Then there was a loud banging on the front door, and a shout 'Police! Open up! Police!' I opened my curtain a fraction and looked out at the road. It was alive with policemen, several with pistols, police-cars and vans. Wright's house opposite was bright with light, and there was a good deal of activity. My first thought was that Hollis was ahead of me in the game, but that Special Branch had been given the wrong address in Cranleigh Gardens. Perhaps I should re-direct the police towards their proper quarry, before Wright and the Russians made good their escape. Then again, perhaps it would be polite to put the Krogers at their ease first. There was no further need for me to remain incognito. I made for the door, and was on the point of calling out that all was well, and there was no cause for alarm, when I realised that the house was full of policemen, and the Krogers were handcuffed together in the hall. Perhaps this was not the moment to intervene: if a mistake had been made, it would doubtless be rectified back at the station. The best thing I could do would be to cross the road and, if possible, keep an eye on Wright. I felt a heavy hand on my shoulder.

'One tiny movement, sir, and the ceiling will be pebble-dashed with your little grey cells.'

'Well done, officer' I said 'Barker, MI5.' I carefully produced my identification.

'That was quick, sir. You'd better have a word with the Superintendent.'

We went downstairs. I smiled reassuringly at the Krogers.

'Double crossing bastard!' said Peter.

'Fascist Pig!' said Helen.

It can't be easy being a New Zealander. I affected not to hear them, and introduced myself to the Superintendent.

'That was quick' he said. 'Didn't think you boys would get here so fast.'

The police were pulling the house apart with little or no regard for the niceties.

'I think you may have made a terrible error of judgement,' I said.

'Bollocks, Barker,' smiled the Superintendent, 'just because you buggers want all the credit. You lot may have got Lonsdale, but Special Branch got the Krogers.'

We picked our way through the wreckage. Floorboards were coming up, walls were coming down. I've never seen such chaos.

'How *did* you get here so fast?' I'd obviously got up the Superintendent's nose. My brain was over-active again. I felt quite dizzy. If the Krogers *were* spies, that put quite a different complexion on the whole business. That would mean that those weren't Slavs opposite, but Watchers. That would explain Wright's behaviour.

'How?' Not a patient man the Superintendent.

'Parachute' I lied distractedly. The most important thing was to make my exit gracefully before Wright turned up. He was obviously expected and would be in a foul mood when he saw what the Police were doing. If he *could* see what they were doing through the gathering dust.

'*Parachute?*' Oh, God. I still hadn't shaken off this bloody man.

'Did I say "Parachute"?' I said innocently. 'That's not very likely is it? Operation PARACHUTE, that's what I was referring to.'

'Never bloody heard of it' snapped the Superintendent.

I tapped the side of my nose. (Another hint from the Manual and rather good.)

'That's all you bloody people want, isn't it? All the effing glory. Well, Mr Barker, I am calling a Press Conference, and I am going to announce to the world that Special Branch has cracked a major Russian spy-ring. Special Branch that is, not you self-satisfied sods in the Secret Service!'

'What the bloody hell's going on here?' Enter left, one of the most self-satisfied sods in the Secret Service. 'Wright. MI5,' added the voice I knew I knew. I backed away into the thick dust-cloud and into a small room off the hall-way. There was a window, but no chance of escape: a policeman stood outside. I knelt down and pretended to be investigating the fire-place.

Wright and the Superintendent were going at it hammer and tongs in the hall. I could only catch snatches of their argument, but I recognised it as an old one. Who was in charge of what?

'This is a security matter.'

'This is a criminal matter.'

'It's an MI5 operation.'

'Call your men off, Superintendent.'

'Get your lot out of here, Wright!'

'I must insist you hand over all available evidence.'

'If you want to look at the evidence – you go through the channels.'

'We need a 48 hour Press black-out.'

'I've called a half-hour Press Conference.'

And so on. And so on. I was suddenly terribly tired of it all. Spy-thatching. What a bloody awful business. I crawled across the floor, and would have fallen asleep, if the door had not opened, a person unknown entered, and slumped into an arm-chair. I heard the rustle of newspaper, so I chanced a glance over the top of the sofa. I hoped whoever it was was on our side. Then again, what side were we one? It was a young fellow I recognised vaguely from the Second Floor of Leconfield House – a junior Watcher. He was having a go at *The Times* crossword. I coughed lightly and introduced myself.

'Eric Griller' he replied. 'Nice and quiet in here.'

'Chaos outside' I said.

'Well, sir, they seem to have finally reached some sort of compromise. We can search the premises, as long as Special Branch keep an eye on us. Not that they've left any evidence to find. They've been stomping about, wreaking havoc, for a good hour now. There isn't a footprint left under size 12. Ha! The plo-od homeward ploughs his weary way!'

'Ploughman' I said.

'I know it's ploughman, sir,' said Grillen, patiently. 'That was a play on words. Thingy's Elegy. In a Country Thing.'

'No,' I said, '12 across. "Goes home late for lunch (9)". Ploughman.'

'Oh, bloody good, sir. Of course, you're Jesmond Barker, I've heard of your genius at the Puzzle.'

'It does play merry hell with your 13 down, where you've got "Xanadu". It now begins with an "L".'

'"Gay pleasure resort", sir. Six letters?'

'Lesbos' I cried.

'Worth a try, sir. How do you spell it?'

I noticed that the policeman was no longer at the window. Perhaps now the moment had come to leave.

'I'm just popping out for a breath of fresh air' I said, opening the window. An image of Captain Oates vainly shouting 'Taxi!' against the Antarctic blizzard flashed before me. I was half-way out when Grillen called out.

'"Ring for gin", sir (9-6)!'

'Telephone Booths' I said.

'Oh, that's terribly good, sir! Bravo!'

'Keep searching' I ordered, and vanished into the night. It was a long walk back from Ruislip to HQ. Heavy drizzle, winds light to moderate.

★   ★   ★

Some days later, I summoned up sufficient courage to beard Hollis in his lair.

'Well done, sir' I said. 'A very successful operation. Lonsdale, Houghton, the Krogers, that's several in the eye for the Russkis.'

'Thank you, Jesmond, yes.' His mind seemed to be else-where. He should have been jumping with joy. 'Yes, a triumph. The Americans are most impressed. A triumph.' He emitted a peal of hollow laughter. 'A *personal* triumph for Mister Peter Wright. Oh, yes.'

'Something amiss, then?'

He threw a fat, pink folder at me. 'Read the bastard's report then Barker. Just you read what Mister bloody Wright has to say about it all.'

'You know I can never make sense of anything Wright writes, sir. He keeps going off into the technical stuff, and Operation this and operation that, and how bloody clever he is. Couldn't you just give it me in a nutshell?'

'In a nutshell, Barker? In a nutshell, he concludes that Moscow knew we were on to Lonsdale from the start. Therefore why, having got him out of the country, did they make him come back? Answer – to protect their agent inside MI5. And given the fact that Lonsdale was of considerable value to them, then their man in MI5 must be very highly placed!' Hollis seemed to be near breaking point. He banged his head angrily on his desk. 'Doesn't he know the words to any other songs, Barker? The man is paranoid! There are Martians in his bathroom!'

Well, I'd been on his case for what seemed years now, and I still couldn't prove anything. But there was still this feeling in the water.

'Congratulations, anyway, sir,' I said. 'I can assure you that morale downstairs has never been higher.'

I left him groaning loudly.

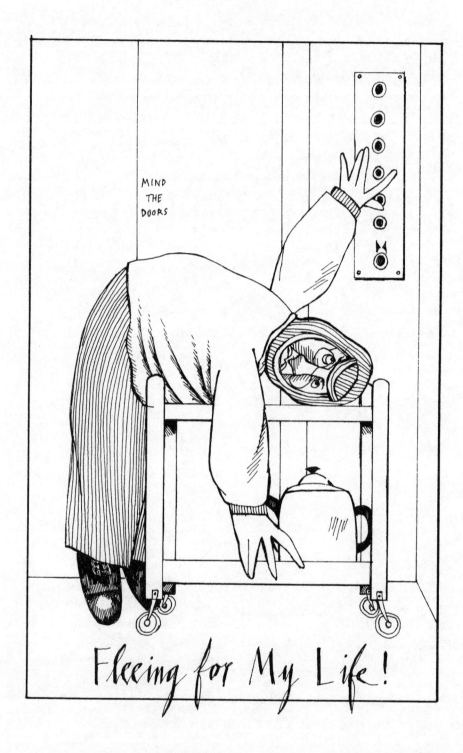

10

Then the shit hit the fan. A high-ranking KGB officer, Anatoli Golitsin, defected and came up with the famous 'Ring of Five'. Five spies, recruited in the 1930s, and all known to each other. The first two were easy – Burgess and Maclean. The third had to be Kim Philby. The fourth was in all probability Sir Anthony Blunt, Surveyor of the Queen's Pictures. The fifth was anybody's guess. Well, we all had our own ideas. Wright had moved out of Leconfield House into the Directorate's HQ in Buckingham Gate. Don't think I wasn't doing a little light probing into the reasons for that.

Philby's case was the first to be looked into. Everyone had known he was a spy for years – but MI6 refused to admit it. It was MI6 who had cleared him. The Interrogation was still played at MI5's Christmas parties. Philby had a formidable stutter which he burst into at the first sign of an embarrassing question. His thoroughly fair and decent interrogators would then finish the sentence for him. Thus was he cleared, and Christmas wouldn't be the same without him at Leconfield House. He had resigned, however, and was now working for the *Observer* in Beirut, and still, according to Golitsin, doing odd jobs for the KGB.

It was Mrs Beardmore who brought it to my attention that Philby and Wright had got on rather well. Wright stuttered too. I imagined that there might be a bond between fellowstutterers. Mrs Beardmore went further and suggested that it would be a simple job for them to swap secrets by stuttering in Morse. It was encouraging to know that the tea-lady was as demented as the rest of us.

I had to some extent recovered from the Ruislip fiasco. No-one had noticed my two-month absence. No-one had known where I was. I was ready now to go into action again.

I was in the immaculate lavatories under Leconfield House, when I heard that scrabbling at the door of my stall that heralded some gobbet of information from Pincher, the lavatory-man.

'Philby's done a bunk' he whispered hoarsely. 'Philby's flown the coop. They've gone bloody mad upstairs.'

'I can't say I'm surprised.' I called back. 'They all knew him. It'd come as something of a shock. I'd feel the same if you or Mrs Beardmore were to suddenly pop up in the Kremlin, smiling broadly and sporting the Order of Lenin.'

I suddenly realised how small my circle of acquaintance was at MI5 and how very few of my colleagues I trusted.

'Pincher!' I cried. 'You were, were you not, a member of the criminal classes prior to your appointment here?'

'That I was, sir.'

'In what particular department did you specialise.'

'Burglarious entry, sir, and on occasion the theft of motor-vehicles.'

'It's the burglary I'm interested in, Pincher. Do you still have the tools of the trade handy?'

'They are at my home in Purley, sir.'

'Bring them in tomorrow, Pincher. We are going to do a job.'

★   ★   ★

I have no idea why I hadn't thought of doing this before. After all he did it all the time. Pincher and I were loitering with intent in Buckingham Gate. A fine pair of rogues we must have looked in the small hours, dressed all in black with Balaclava helmets and Pincher's clanking bag. There was a thick drizzle.

A passing policeman stopped and shone his torch at us.

'And where would we be going, gentlemen?'

'We're – we're – we're –' said Pincher.

'Waiting for a taxi?' suggested the helpful constable.

'Yes' I said, 'we've – um – been – er –'

'To a Fancy Dress Ball, I imagine, sir.'

'Indeed, officer' I replied. 'As – as – as –'

'As members of that fine body of men, sir, the SAS.'

'Absolutely, officer. Well done!' He could have interrogated Philby. He had a natural talent for this sort of thing. He saluted us and went on his way whistling the theme from *Z-Cars*.

Pincher was shaking like a leaf.

'Come on Pincher,' I said sharply, 'pull yourself together, and let's get inside.' There was only one light on in the building and that was on the Fourth Floor.

Pincher pulled himself together. Only his head shook.

'That's a nasty looking door. I don't know; I don't know at all.'

While he was grumbling to himself and fossicking about in his large canvas bag, I gave the door a gentle push. It slowly opened.

'Hello chaps,' said a voice from the dark vestibule, 'Simon Freake. DBSO.'

I had no idea what that meant. Probably nothing. There were a number of jobs like that about in the Secret Service. To tell the truth, I had one, but nobody had ever given me any initials. Nor for that matter had anyone ever told me what section I belonged to. My stipend, I had discovered, was written off in a variety of ways – as window-cleaning, and vehicle maintenance.'

'You're the Ordnance fellows, then?' said Freake, jumping to a conclusion – an occupational hazard in MI5.

'Yes, sir,' I replied.

'Come to test the vests, etcetera. Where's the porker?'

'I'm sorry, sir?' *Operation* PORKER, perhaps. An oblique reference to the police?

'Not to worry.' Freake was a blithe spirit. 'We can borrow a horse.' He ushered us in.

'Like a drink first?' he asked, as he led us down a lengthy corridor. 'Scotch? Coffee?' I noticed that Pincher had been bright enough to leave his bag on the doorstep. We settled for Johnnie Walker in plastic cups.

'Come down then, chaps.' He opened a door in the wall, and

led us down to the basement. Cellars, to be more precise, and sizeable too. So this was the Range I'd heard about. There were targets in the distance. I could see snarling men in fur hats painted on them, and a huge sandpit surrounded by sandbags. Turning, I got the fright of my life. There was a sizeable audience. All male, either in evening dress or uniform, masses of decorations. It could have been some Embassy binge, save for the subdued lighting and the plastic cups.

'Right, gentlemen!' cried Freake. 'My *lords* and gentlemen!' He corrected himself with a giggle. 'We are ready.' He turned to Pincher and myself. 'Get those on, chaps.' He pointed to a couple of padded waistcoats on a tressle table. 'And down the far end with you, eh?' He clapped us both on the back, and drifted off towards the brass.

'Colonel, I wonder if you'd do the honours?'

The Colonel looked as though he had drained quite a number of plastic cups. He lurched a little as Freake handed him some massive weapon. Pincher and I set off through the sand towards the targets. I found myself singing 'Goodbye' from *The White Horse Inn*. I was not to know how appropriate was my choice of number.

'I'll join the Legion that's what I'll do' I sang.

'What?' said Pincher.

'I was singing' I said.

'Oh.' said Pincher. And after a pause he enquired. 'What are we doing?'

I looked back down the range and there, some fifty yards or so away, lit by a single naked bulb dangling from the vaulted ceiling, stood the Colonel, armed and unsteady.

'I hope,' I said, 'that we are modelling these waistcoats for those gentlemen up the other end there.' I twirled round a couple of times so that they could enjoy my waistcoat more fully.

'Keep still, you bastard!' bawled the Colonel.

'That's not it' said Pincher, buttoning his waistcoat to the neck. I shared his unease. 'That bugger's going to shoot at us with that fucking great thing.' It *was* a monstrous weapon. Armour-piercing, I'd have said, though I wasn't going to say as much to Pincher.

'Ready?' called Freake.

'Stand still, you shits!' That was the Colonel.

'Fire!' cried Freake.

And there was a series of fearsome explosions, and I had sufficient time to register that Pincher's head had come off, before I was hit a most violent blow in the chest and thrown backwards some fifteen yards into the cellar wall. I slid slowly down the wall – I was some twenty feet up it – and sat there in a state of total shock.

'Bugger me' I whispered. 'Bugger me for an old soldier.'

And Pincher's head which lay beside me seemed to nod, before it fell on its side. I also registered that he had died looking none too pleased.

Freake and the Colonel were padding towards us through the sand.

'The damned fool moved.' The Colonel was livid. 'He must have ducked. The damned fool. Now his head's come off. Serve him right.'

'How are you?' Freake asked of me.

'Still alive, I think,' I replied. I could have done with a second opinion.

'Have a drop of this.' Freake poured a plastic cupful of Scotch down my throat. I coughed violently. My chest hurt.

'You,' said the Colonel, 'had the good sense to stay still. *He*, silly bugger, moved.'

'Just lie there, old fellow,' said Freake. I had no other plans. 'We have more work to do,' continued Freake. 'Come, Colonel. Pincher's body was brought over and laid out near his head. Freake knelt down beside me.

'See this,' he said, and held a lump of sugar under my nose. Was I expected to eat it? I shook my head. 'Now watch' he said, and springing to his feet he bounded over to a surly horse that stood where Pincher and I had been. He fed the lump of sugar to the horse, and began to run like a hairy goat back towards the be-medalled audience.

'Ten! – nine! – eight!' he counted as he fled. 'Seven!'

The horse exploded into a million lumps as he cried 'Six!' Most of the lumps headed brass-wards. The late Pincher and I were spared most of the unpleasantness. I flicked bits of smouldering horse-meat from my trousers, and brushed an eyeball from Pincher's forehead, before realising it was his.

I had quite forgotten why I had come here in the first place. I too had work to do, and this would seem as good a moment as any to do it. There was a fine chaos at the other end of the cellar. The previously resplendent assembly now looked like a gala night in the abattoir. What a supremely disgusting spectacle, I thought as I staggered towards them, extremely dazed, very pissed and hurting considerably. As I looked at the blood and gut-covered congregation, I swore purblind that meat would never pass my lips again. Nor has it, I may add. I dropped the waistcoat at the door, and made my way slowly and painfully upstairs. I only hoped that that bang in the chest had done no permanent damage. I had to find Wright's office quickly, before I passed out. My health, as you may have gathered, has never been very good, and I can easily do without being struck by anti-Tank missiles. I remember thinking, though, they must be jolly pleased with the waistcoat.

★   ★   ★

My luck was in again. It had certainly been fluctuating all night. I found a crude map in the reception area, and there was Wright's office on the Third Floor. I took the lift. There was little chance of discovery. Everyone who was anyone was in the cellar sloshing about in ruined attire, totally apalled at the horror of it all. The horse, I imagine, was no more delighted than Pincher. Freake, of course, would be busy preparing the cover-up. In fact, Pincher's head and body were discovered under a hedge near Londonderry a week later, and the entire thing blamed on the IRA. There isn't even a plaque in his place of business.

Wright's door was locked, but I had brought a bunch of skeleton keys and the fourth one fitted. I turned on his desk-lamp and sat down heavily. All I really wanted to do was go to bed. I took off my Balaclava and determined to concentrate. I put on my glasses and into focus swam a bulging file, covered in stamps and stickers – TOP SECRET, FOR MY EYES ONLY, KEEP OUT! And there, in the middle, in Wright's spidery hand 'The Fifth Man?'. I found my Minox camera and began the laborious business of photographing every page. This took an hour, at the end of which I was so deeply fatigued that I replaced my Balaclava, crawled under the desk and fell into a deep sleep.

I awoke to find that I was not alone under the desk. I shared the space with Wright's baggy pinstripes. I was stiff as a board, and almost screamed as a spasm of cramp shot through my left leg. Any movement, however, was quite out of the question. I resigned myself to a long, hard day under a desk. I made myself as comfortable as I could, without disturbing his legs. They never moved. At one stage I thought he might have died, but then I heard the rasping of his pen above. Occasionally he would pick up his headphones and I would hear the squawk of static as he checked out one of his many buggings. It made very dull listening. What fascinated me was that no-one came to see him in his office. And no-one telephoned him. Sandwiches and coffee were brought in for him at lunchtime, and I realised how very hungry I was. The afternoon dragged on, he wrote, he listened, he muttered to himself, but I couldn't understand a word. Then suddenly he picked up the telephone. I nearly jumped out of my skin.

'Victor? Victor' said Wright. Code-name obviously. Victor Victor or was it just Victor? 'It's not Mitchell,' Wright sounded distraught, 'More months of bloody hard work down the drain. It's not Mitchell.'

What Mitchell wasn't it? I was quite dizzy with pain and fatigue. Mitchell? *Leslie* Mitchell, the suave Television Announcer? *Guy* Mitchell, the popular American crooner? 'She wears red feathers and a hooley-hooley skirt', my brain was giddy with song, but I could barely hear it for the bassoons and tympani emanating from my empty stomach. *George* Mitchell, the Chocolate-Coloured Coon? Was no-one to be trusted? Mitchell? Ah, Mitchell! Hollis's Deputy. The Deputy D-G. So, it wasn't *that* Mitchell? What wasn't?

Wright was now explaining down the telephone in that patronising tone he would adopt with laymen that there was no way in which *his* telephone or office could be bugged, and that they could talk without fear, and talk they must, or talk I certainly must, he said, and now he was pleading to Victor, the only man he had even really admired, his hero, his patron, please listen to me, please Victor. The man was cracking up, but not as fast as I was. He was now talking far too quickly and far too softly for my one good ear, which since the explosions of the night was half the ear it was, to make any sense of it. Fortunately, as he spoke, pieces of paper floated down from above, and once I had found my glasses I was able to deduce that they contained the bones of his relentless monologue.

The first sheet was a list of operations in which he had been involved since the mid-50s. Operations with lunatic names like CHOIR and MOLE, DEW-WORM and PIG ROOT. All cock-ups. Double-agent cases – some 20 of those. All worthless. All the stuff about the Watchers. And Lonsdale. And Philby. Give him his due, he admitted there could be good and valid reasons why they had all been disasters but then he'd crossed out the admission and writen in red pencil – High-level Penetration. He liked that phrase.

Another piece of paper simply contained five names – Hollis, Mitchell, Charlie Orange, Winterborn, Myself. 'Myself' was firmly crossed out again in red. Winterborn, an old sidekick of his, was crossed out in black. Charlie Orange simply had 'Too bloody stupid! beside his name, which I thought was a bit strong. Mitchell had two questionmarks against him and the world 'sly'. Hollis, one question-mark and quite a wordy critique – 'aloof, pedestrian autocrat'.

Wright had raised his voice now so I made a rude ear-trumpet out of the two sheets of paper and thrust it up between his knees.

'I knew it was one of them, Victor, but which? I thought Mitchell the best bet. I certainly knew whichever it was was on to me. You know my methods. When I put my files away at night in the safe, I mark the corners with a pencil. They were moved, Victor. And by one of *them*, for only two others have access to my safe, only two men know all the combinations, the D-G and his Deputy, Victor. How do these apples grab you, baby? The Great Goat-head is abroad in the Corridors of Power, the cloven-hoof is hopping over our Axminster, there is a foul stench of brimstone in my secret places. We must root out Beelzebub!' And so on. It was slowly dawning on me, and I was not going to hurry the process as my head hurt quite enough already, that if he had given up on Mitchell, then he would now be turning his attention to Hollis, and I, the last remains of Jesmond Barker, would be caught in the cross-fire and in no condition to bob or weave.

'I mean we gave Mitchell the works,' whined Wright. 'All

right, we got off to a slow start because Hollis wouldn't let us go the whole hog, but we bugged his office, put a two-way mirror in, had the closed-circuit television on him, and then when we got Dick White to put a little MI6 pressure on Hollis, and he relented, we had MI6 Watchers following him, we fed him some shit-hot intelligence he was bound to pass on. All right he didn't, in fact he hardly read it, I'm simply saying we did all we could. Of course, he knew he was being followed in the end, he didn't know his arse from his elbow, didn't know what was happening to him – the man was visibly cracking, Victor. I watched him through the mirror, Victor, he looked bloody awful and that's when we should have given him a thorough grilling, but Hollis wouldn't sanction it. Hollis wouldn't let us approach the CIA, see if they had anything on Mitchell, he said it wasn't their business. Well, I'm sorry, Victor but I'm thoroughly pissed off.'

Not, I thought, as the toes of my left foot flamed and fizzed with pain, as pissed off as I am. The full implications of what they had done to Mitchell were beginning to sink into the porridge-like remnants of my grey cells. If they could behave that ruthlessly to an old colleague on the brink of retirement, simply on a whim and a half-baked theory, God knows what they would do to me. Particularly if they found me crouched under Peter Wright's desk with Minox and reading-glasses.

'Let me tell you what finally convinced me, Victor. The Moment of Truth, as it were. I was reporting to Hollis nightly. He was friendly enough. We talked of his time in China, his visit to Moscow during the 30s. We would often ransack Mitchell's office together. Well, I would do the work, Hollis would sit at Mitchell's desk with a drink and tell me extremely dirty jokes. He has a vast collection of them. I am getting to the point, Victor, I'm sorry, I realise you want to get back to your spermatozoa. Yes, I apologise, you know I worship the ground you tread upon. So daintily, may I add, for a man of your proportions. Yes, sir, this is it.'

What an extraordinary relationship this is, I thought. I must look into Victor. He may well be the key. I must try and remember his name. Oh dear, thick fog had descended in the brain.

'There was a desk, Victor, in Mitchell's office. Two of the drawers were locked, so I asked Hollis for his permission to pick them. This he gave. He told me that the desk had belonged to Guy Liddell. Yes, Victor, a giant of the legend of MI5. Deputy D-G after the War. I know that, thank you, Victor.'

I was glad they were providing sub-titles.

'Well, Victor, next evening I brought my tools along and opened the two drawers. Empty, Victor, but small marks in one of them revealed to my keen, trained eye that an object had recently been removed from that drawer, and there were scratch marks in the lock, as if the drawer had been opened recently.'

Well, it had, you silly bugger, I almost shouted at Wright, by *you*, you sanctimonious twit.

'Hollis was as surprised as I when I showed him. Then, Victor, as I said, the Moment of Truth. Only Hollis and I knew I was going to open that drawer. Hollis is our man, Victor.'

Oh, God, here we go again, I thought. Wright rang off, after paying a further series of lavish compliments to Victor. I had no idea what the time was, or the date for that matter, but surely Wright had a home to go to. I was greatly encouraged when he went to his safe and put his files away. Yes, he did mark their position with a pencil. How lucky I was that he had forgotten to go through this ritual last night. Perhaps the Mitchell business had blown him temporarily off course. An attack of conscience perhaps? Never, I thought. He had one final listen in his earphones, turned off his equipment, and was gone. How on earth was I to leave? Very, very slowly I levered myself out from under the desk. The legs straightened, though there was little feeling in them. My back would *not* straighten, I could not raise my body from the waist up, it remained firmly parallel to the floor. I thought of ringing for an ambulance, and bluffing it out, but I might well be caught, and I remembered Manslaughter's reference all those years ago to the Eleventh Commandment.

Painfully, I made my way to the door, outside which, as luck would have it was a tea-trolley identical to Mrs Beardmore's. I removed the empty urn and rested the upper length of my body on the top of it. I had wheels. I stuffed some stale buns into my pocket. I had food. With feeble movements of my legs I propelled myself towards the lift. Again, my luck held, no-one worked late at the Directorate – they had cocktail parties to attend, and fat dinners with Ambassadors. The lift-doors opened automatically so entry was easy enough, but I was unable to look up at the buttons and inadvertently I pressed the Alarm. Angry bells went off. I pressed the next button up and was heading south. Too far. The gates opened and I could tell from the sandy floor that I was back in the basement. God, they're good, I thought, not a trace of the exploding horse or the horrors of the night. Fresh sand everywhere as far as I could see, and the sweet smell of some commercial air-freshener. I could hear the noise of studded boots on the stone steps. Down which Pincher and I had been ushered the previous night. With my fingers I counted three buttons up and pressed again. This was better. The gates opened at the ground floor, and ahead of me I could see that the front door was open. Freedom beckoned. One snag, however: between myself and Buckingham Gate stood a policeman, truncheon drawn. I pressed my feet against the back wall of the lift, and pushed myself off like an Olympic breast-stroker on the turn. The trolley, given added impetus by three steps down to the tiled floor of the hall, knocked the officer out of the way with casual ease. Through the front door I shot, down the steps, and I would have vanished under the traffic in Buckingham Gate, had the trolley not struck a lamp-post and disintegrated under me. I lay in the wreckage, ignored by passers-by. This is the English way, and quite proper in my view. The bottom shelf of the tea-trolley was still in one piece, and so were the wheels attached to it. As quickly as I could I knelt on this and Porgy-like, using my fists for propulsion, I set off towards the Mall.

I was only approached once by a member of the public on the long, painful trip to Leconfield House. I sang a chorus of 'Bess, You Is my Woman Now' to him, and was the proud recipient of five shillings.

How I made it to my office in Leconfield House, I am uncertain. I passed in and out of consciousness. I remember lying in the empty lobby pushing the stale buns into my mouth, trying to summon the last of my strength for the final assault on the staircase. In the office, I lay on my back, legs straight up in the air, and fell into the deepest sleep I can ever remember.

The sun awoke me, flashing intermittently into my eyes through the Venetian blinds. And there standing above me, holding a polystyrene cup of something, was, of all people, Mitchell.

'My God,' he said, 'I thought I was bad, but what, in Heaven's name, have they done to you?'

I must have presented a fearsome sight, lying there, bent into a perfect 'L', covered in bits of horse, a pinch of Pincher, sand and crumbs, unshaven and bruised, my Balaclava helmet back to front. Mitchell knelt, and reversed my Balaclava.

'It's you, Barker. Good Lord, I thought you were dead.'

'You look none too well yourself,' I croaked. They'd reduced him to ashes. Grey-faced, red-eyed and haggard, he was not the man I remembered.

'The bastards!' he said.

'Ditto' I replied, gamely, as he forced either tea or coffee down me. It was always hard to tell with Mrs Beardmore. If peas floated on the surface, it was soup. Probably.

'No,' he said, 'if I'm surprised to see you still alive, or very nearly, it's only that there were rumours of an "accident" on the Range, and your name was mentioned.'

I was not so far gone that I could not detect quotation marks.

'Accident?' I said. 'You mean I was set up?'

'Oh, yes' said Mitchell. 'Freake was there, I imagine?'

I nodded and squealed with pain.

'Gascoyne Balls?' asked Mitchell. 'The Colonel?'

'Oh.' The memory was jogged. 'Colonel Balls. He was there. I didn't recognise him. I met him years ago. He shot Pincher's head off.'

'He's licensed to kill' said Mitchell. 'Almost anybody he likes. Well, someone's got it in for you. Been treading on any toes?'

'Just keeping my eyes open' I replied. 'And that's a job in itself.'

'What branch are you in?' asked Mitchell. I shook my head, and regretted that immediately. 'You're right.' he said. 'Less I know the better.'

'You're off the hook' I said. 'If it's any comfort, you're cleared.'

'Bit bloody late' he said, and sighed deeply. 'Once they've done you over, that's it for life. The name is mud. Fine end to a career, eh? Buggered end to end in the last lap. Ha, bloody, ha!'

I could not blame him for feeling bitter. But at least they probably wouldn't try to kill him. I was on the hit-list. No place to be with a superbly trained animal like Colonel Balls in pursuit. And Hollis? I must warn him.

'There won't be an Intelligence Agency in the world that won't believe I'm a traitor' said Mitchell sadly. 'They'll have put out the word. And once out, that's it, Barker, that is it.' And with that he left, and I never saw him again.

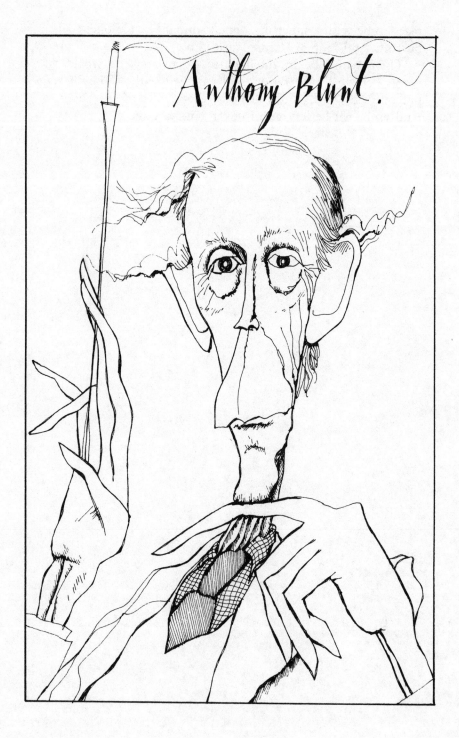

11

'Why didn't you tell me about poor Mitchell? And you telling Wright it was OK to investigate him?' I was thoroughly irked, and I think Hollis recognised the fact. 'And helping him search? And telling him filthy stories?'

'I'm sorry, Barker' he said, 'but it was a question of morale. Had it leaked out that Wright was being investigated, well, on top of Burgess, Maclean and Philby, quite frankly it would have been more than the Service could have borne.'

'I see that, sir' I replied. 'Then again I'm sorry that you did not trust me sufficiently to impart such information to me.'

'So am I' said Hollis. 'but in this profession one trusts no-one.'

'And that you felt you could not tell me filthy stories,' I added sadly.

'That was an oversight, Barker, and for that I apologise. Sit down, and I'll tell you a couple I picked up in China before the War.'

They were absolutely foul, but amusing enough. He told me that there was nothing else to do in China in the 30s (he was working for the American Tobaco Company) except drink and trade dirty jokes. I felt that I had now created a suitable atmosphere into which to unbottle the big one.

'There is a growing feeling, sir, in the Service that you are, to put mildly, an agent for the KGB'. There, I'd said it.

Hollis sat down. I'd caught him on the hop there. Quiet

desperation suddenly became noisy desperation. He was back on his feet.

'Good God!' he roared. 'Peter bloody Wright, is it?'

I nodded.

'The cheek of the man!' cried Hollis. 'And all the time I thought *he* was.'

'How do we stop him?' I asked.

'There's no stopping him, Jesmond. He rolls on, right or wrong, like some great juggernaut, crushing everything in his path. Look at the state of poor Mitchell.' He poured himself a large drink, and knocked it back in one. 'So' he exhaled, 'I'm next.' He refilled his glass. 'Have we any idea what evidence he has?'

Feeling rather pleased with myself, I handed him my Minox. Hollis observed dryly that there was no film in it. Sometimes I wondered if I was really cut out for the Great Game. To restore myself a little in his eye, I asked him casually if the name 'Victor' meant anything to him. I was astonished at his reaction. A sudden pallor. A third drink, and a fourth.

'Hands off!' he ordered. 'Don't touch. Not that one. Not Victor.'

I knew better than to push him. I could always drink deep at that fount of wisdom, Mrs Beardmore. I made to leave, but he called after me.

'Just one question, Barker. They are now satisfied that Mitchell isn't a spy. And yet my behaviour during that investigation convinces them that I am one – the fact that I refused to believe them, that I was reluctant to authorise technical facilities, that I wouldn't allow them to interrogate him, that I didn't brief the CIA and Hoover until late in the case. This is the question, Barker: if I am your Fifth Man, would it not have best served my interests to have had Mitchell pronounced a spy and thrown him into the Tower or what-ever?'

'Yes' I said, 'but that's not how their minds work.'

I went off to see if I could find Mrs Beardmore. I heard her long before I saw her. A mournful wailing. When I came upon her she was in a small alcove by the Emergency Exit on the third floor. She half-sat, half-lay beside her tea-trolley, dabbing at her eyes with her apron and crying hysterically. I gave her a couple of sharp cuffs, and this seemed to steady her.

'What is it, Mrs Beardmore?' Perhaps she had been declared redundant. The Service was always looking for cutbacks.

'It's awful, Mr Barker, I can't believe it – it's so awful. That lovely man, Mr Barker, so gracious, he always had his own tea, Orange Pekoe, and his own beautiful china. And now – oh, Mr Barker.' And off she went again. I poured her a mugful of her own strong brew.

'What has happened to whom?' I asked gently. 'Sir Anthony Blunt' she spluttered 'That fine gentleman. Who else could wear mauve socks to advantage? He's – he's confessed.' She looked at me dramatically.

'He's come out of the closet?'

'He's a spy.'

The Fourth Man, of course. There had been grave doubts about him since Burgess and Maclean took off, but his confession would put the cat among the pigeons, particularly if it went public. I made a start by closing the window above Mrs Beardmore.

'He was a sweetheart!' she declared, bosoms heaving. 'A pussycat!'

I left her shouting his references, and headed back towards Hollis's office, to see if there was anything I could do in the light of Blunt's confession. As I entered the outside office I saw Wright going into Hollis's room, and heard his surprised cry of 'Victor!' The plot, in my view, thickened. I got into a cupboard and waited. It was not long before Wright came out again at his dogged plod, shaking his head and muttering. As soon as he was out of sight, I leaped out of the cupboard and headed for Hollis's office, determined to have a glimpse of Victor. Hollis did not seem at all surprised to see me.

'You've heard then about Anthony?'

I nodded. I was not going to reveal my source.

'We're all terribly shocked, of course.' That was Victor. He reminded me very much of Sidney Greenstreet. I was tempted to say that I had no idea as to the whereabouts of the Maltese Falcon. He also looked as if he had been crying.

'Victor Rothschild, this is Jesmond Barker, one of our agents.' Is that what I was? What was Victor? 'Victor was a great friend of Anthony's for thirty years or more. He has only just heard the news.'

'We were at Cambridge together and I was his landlord during the war. Anthony and Guy Burgess lived together in a little house of mine in Bentinck Street. He was also very close to my wife. She lived there too. She will be dreadfully upset.'

'Tess, Victor's wife, and Victor served MI5 with great distinction throughout the war. Victor won the George Medal, no less. Fellow of the Royal Society, botanist, geologist, very few pies Victor hasn't had a finger in politics, intelligence, banking and he is a great admirer of Peter Wright.'

'First-rate chap' said Victor, 'and thoroughly decent. I've asked him to break the news to Tess about Anthony. He's said he will. So kind. Excuse me.' And tottering on the brink of tears again, he left Hollis's office. I shall most certainly, I thought, run our Victor through Mrs Beardmore when she's recovered.

'Get to Blunt, Barker, before Wright does. Tell him to stall. We do not want this business out in the open. Ye Gods, Macmillan and Co. are just about recovering from Profumo and if this slips out – it could mean curtains. Curtains for all of us, Barker, because who is riding high in the polls? Who is ready and eager to form the next Government? Harold Wilson, Barker. God help us all.' And he tapped the side of his nose, hummed 'The Red Flag' loudly and poured himself a drink. 'We all know about Harold' he added meaningfully.

'You want *me* to see Blunt?'

Hollis snapped back into action. 'Yes' he replied, 'Nine o'clock tomorrow morning at the Courtauld Institute. He's expecting you, of course, and I've cleared it with the Palace. Her Majesty has been informed and has given us *Carte blanche*.'

'Righty ho, sir.' I had a feeling I was finally going to make some sort of impact on the Service. 'Should I go and look up all that 30s stuff in the Registry?'

'Have you ever seen the state of all the 30s stuff in the Registry?'

'No, Sir.'

'Oh, it's horrid. The Boche dropped a bomb on it in the War, and what remains is all black and tacky and comes apart in your hands. One word of warning, Barker, and this one's straight from the Palace. Do not ask Blunt about a visit he made to Germany after the War on behalf of the Palace. Not a word. Do not enquire. Strictly speaking, they say, it is not relevant.'

106

Oh, my sweet Lord, what are we getting into now? Who are we covering up here? The Duke of Windsor? Edward the Seventh? Don't ask, Barker. Don't ask.

★ ★ ★

'Come!' I obeyed the brittle coo-ee, and entered Blunt's sanctum at the Courtauld with some trepidation. His study was a magnificent room, bags of gold leaf and paintings as precious as the man himself, he had perhaps based the design on an extravagant chapel in the Kremlin. The air was heavy with a musky aroma, but my old nose is as reliable as my deaf ear, on which he fell. It is the only time in my life that a man has put his tongue in my ear, all I could think of in response was to ask rather lamely that a window be opened.

'Just testing,' he said playfully, and directed me to an armchair beside the fireplace. He was immaculate in a pale grey double breasted suit, a pink tie with massive knot matching his socks. He reclined gracefully on an ottoman opposite. There was a small table between us on which stood a charming tea-service and 'petits-fours'. I put my machine on it. Such was the importance of my mission, for which I kept reminding myself I was pathetically ill-qualified, that Hollis had insisted I visit the Quarter Master. I imagined he would issue me with lumps of sugar that blew up horses, a watch that turned into a miniature helicopter, a lighter fuelled by CS gas, an inflatable woman that would cause a Pope to pause long enough for you to overpower him. Not so. 'This is the latest thing' he had said, handing me this book-sized machine.

'It's a tape-recorder of some sort' I said.

'It looks like a tape-recorder of some sort' replied the QM smugly, 'but, in fact, it is a lie-detector.'

'Good Lord' I said.

I asked Blunt if he would mind if I recorded our conversation – one should never overlook the common courtesies.

'That's a lie-detector' he smiled, 'I've seen it advertised in *Big Business Today*.

'No, its not' I said sharply, and the machine emitted a mocking whinny.

'It's just a tape-recorder' I cried, trying to drown further appalling electronic shrieks.

'Do I detect the dainty hand of Petronella?' Blunt giggled.

'Who?' I said, which at least silenced the machine.

'Peter Wright' whispered Blunt. 'Tricky little fellow our Petronella.'

'No' I replied sharply. Off went the machine again. OK, I thought, so it was a product of his dainty hand.

'He's coming to see me tomorrow.' Blunt inserted another pale blue cigarette into his ivory holder. 'To know him is to love him, eh, Jesmond?'

'Oh, yes' I said, and the machine had the decency to whirr, whoop twice and explode. I realised that I was in the presence of a True Professional.

'I imagine,' continued Blunt, blowing perfect smoke-rings upwards at the ornate ceiling, 'that the dear boy is at this moment at work with his little Black and Decker, drilling through the wall.' He waved towards the grate: 'About there, I would imagine.' He pointed to a spot beside some finely engraved tongs. At that precise moment, a little shower of plaster fell on to the carpet. We both laughed. He put his immaculately manicured finger to his lips.

'Not to worry, Jezebel, dearest,' he said. 'He won't have it in operation until tomorrow. We can do what we like.' And he winked at me boldly. Well, one of us was enjoying himself, and it wasn't Jezebel Barker.

'I suppose you want to know all about Betty Burgess and Molly Maclean and dear old Fenella Philby.'

'On the contrary, Mr Blunt' I replied stolidly, 'the less I know the better. Roger Hollis –'

'Darling Henrietta!' trilled Blunt.

'Roger Hollis' I persevered, 'is keen to play for time. The appearance of a Fourth Man suddenly at this particular moment in our History could be extremely damaging to the National Interest.' I had rehearsed that sentence all night and considered it rather good.

'I bet you'd love to know why I went to Germany just after the War ended, wouldn't you?'

'No, I certainly would not' I lied, thanking God that the bloody machine was *kaput*.

'There are any number of fascinating things I could tell you.' He poured me another cup of tea, without even removing his bright-blue eyes from mine. Well, I remember them as bright blue, he certainly had a way about him.

'What Roger would like, and he will trade immunity for this, is for you to stall Wright. Take it slowly, give him a little at a time, but keep him at it for as long as you possibly can.'

'Dear heart,' said Blunt, 'I am never at a loss for words. I shall chat away contentedly of this and that for years and years. Oh, I can think of delicious little gobbets I can throw his way. Pink herrings that will have him running round and round in ever-decreasing spy-rings. I can give him names. There are one or two spies I've never liked. They are, in the main, very unpleasant people. But then it's a simply horrid business, isn't it sordid, Jezzy?'

I nodded. He nestled back among the plump cushions on the ottoman.

'It was all wonderfully exciting when I signed on. Those were the salad days of Russian Intelligence. The Great Illegals they were called, isn't that sweet? Trotskyites who truly believed in nothing more than International Communism and the Comintern. They created spy-rings all over Wendy World. Brilliant men, so clever, so cultured, such fun to know, believe me, dear, they were artists, so different from the awful brutes you have today. Stella Stalin had them all done away with in '38. He thought they were all plotting against him. Nasty Trots! Are you paranoid, darling? If not, you soon will be. It goes with the job. I was always glad I had my other loves to fall back on. Have you another love to fall back on?'

He laughed gaily at my discomfiture. 'Another *interest*.'

I looked out of the window. There was a heavy drizzle.

'The weather' I said. 'I've always found that strangely fascinating. I know it's not everybody's idea of –'

'No, dear' yawned Blunt, 'but no-one's perfect. Still, how-ever dull, duckie, cling to it. Never become obsessed, sweetie. That way lies madness. I always, thanks be to Glenda God, always had my art. I never really got on with the KGB when they took over after the War, so unlike the absolute loves who ran us in the '30s, they were –' his lightly coloured lips pursed, and I thought he was going to spit into the scuttle – 'they were bureaucrats, technocrats no time at all for the good things of life.' He laid his hand briefly on my thigh and then picked up a little biscuit. 'Heigh ho, Jezzy, *chacun à son pouf!*'

He could, as he had advertised, certainly chat. We moved on to gin, and he talked of Cambridge and the Apostles, and the joys of being young and homosexual and Communist. I remember remarking sadly that I had never been any of those things. I also recall taking him to task quite severely.

'This is all very well,' I cried, gesturing to the expensive trappings that engulfed us, 'but you *were* a spy. You betrayed your country. You betrayed fellow-countrymen of yours. You caused their deaths.'

'They were spies, too,' said Blunt. 'It happens. One was always aware that one might come to a sticky end. Spies are a truly International Brotherhood, Jezzy. They are above Country, beyond Government, they spend as much time pursuing each other as they do their Nation's enemies. That's as true of the KGB as it is of MI5.'

He agreed to go along with our plot. I think he quite looked forward to it. Perhaps he had been surveying the Queen's pictures too long, and needed a little of the cut and thrust of the Great Game.

'I don't think Petronella will approve of me. I'm all the things he dislikes most, but perhaps he will fall a little in love with me. I shall be at my most fascinating. And if he comes the heavy. – Wow! Don't worry Jezzy, you're in safe hands.'

As it turned out, I was. He kept Wright occupied for the next six years or more. He dropped tit-bits that sent Wright off to the Registry for months, checking and re-checking thousands of files. He suggested Wright talk to the likes of Isaiah Berlin and Arthur Marshall, not spies at all, but cheerful gossips who would regale him with spicy tales of Cambridge in the '30s – who did what, and with which and to whom – for weeks upon end. And he fed him some genuine spies, silly little men, who in their turn fattened Wright's files with a diet of Red Herring and Wild Goose. And round and round he went, Oxford, Cambridge, America, France. There were casualties, of course, during his investigation of the Oxford Ring, two suspects, one an MP, committed suicide and a third had a heart attack. That had to be hushed-up sharpish. Luckily, that occurred at the end of the lengthy inquiry, the vetting of a generation.

I only ever went through Wright's office twice. I've described the first time, eighteen hours under his desk. The second time was at the end of the 60s when I was deeply into the Great Conspiracy Theory. That's where I picked up that phrase, 'the vetting of a generation'. It was on the cover of a file in his Out tray. He always liked grandiose titles. There was one sheet of paper inside listing the achievements of this six-year vetting.

(1) We know every member of the Ring of Five
(2) We have discovered one spy previously unknown.
(3) We have discovered 40 probable spies, alive or dead.
(4) We have probed the records of dozens of people in every sphere of public life. Most were clean.
(5) We know our History, and need never be afraid again.
(6) We have exorcised the past.

I should have retired after my chat with Anthony Blunt. I didn't know it then, but that was my Golden Hour. We all have one, I'm told. So how did I spend the next six years while Wright imitated the actions of the Oojah-Bird? Well, instead of heading for the dizzy heights, which I should have done after registering my first success at twenty-odd years, I'm afraid it was downhill all the way. In heavy drizzle. I got the wrong end of the stick entirely. Heaven knows, it's easily done in our business. My major error was to ignore Blunt's excellent words of advice – 'Never become obsessed, sweetie.' Maybe it is something of a tribute to my strength of character that it took twenty-odd years in the Secret Service for me to become certifiable, but it also points to a sorry lack of judgement, that I was unable to spot the symptoms.

Inspired by my success, in which, in retrospect, I was only the middle-man between Blunt and Hollis, but highly delighted with myself, I determined to look into the mysterious Victor Rothschild.

It is extraordinary how quickly one can prepare a case against someone, if the mood is upon you. Two visits to the Registry, and a cup of tea and three macaroons with Mrs Beardmore was ample, and Rothschild was doomed. If we had even flirted with the notion that Peter Wright was the KGB's man in MI5, then, my word, he was St Francis of Assisi, Mother Theresa and Cliff Richard compared to Victor Rothschild.

A 'leftie' for most of his life, an ardent Russophile during the

War when he worked for MI5, arguing vigorously for greater access for Moscow to information obtained by our Secret Services, landlord to Burgess and Blunt, husband to Tess, and MI5 officer who has shared those digs with Burgess and Blunt, friend of Aneurin Bevan, patron of *Tribune*, the red rag, and sole hero of Peter Wright. Ho! Ho! Ho!

Hollis was close to retirement. What a spelndid gift my report would be. I scorned the Lift and ran up the stairs to his Office. He was sitting at this desk, nursing a whisky. I tossed my report in front of him.

He pushed it away from him.

'It's a funny old world, Jesmond Barker, a funny old world. Just had Peter in. I think he came to say "Goodbye," but he never said it. I started off with some idle chatter about retiring, the fact that the pension was rotten, that I would divide my time between golfing and walking, that sort of thing. I told him how strange I felt to think that in a few weeks my portrait would be up on the wall with Kell, Petrie, Sillitoe and Dick White. Then I thought "Why not?" and I said right out loud, straight to his face – "Peter, why do you think I'm a spy?"'

I was astounded. 'Good God' I said. 'That's asking him. What did the old bastard say to that?'

He looked at his watch and sighed. 'Three hours it took him, and he was talking quite quickly. All the old stuff, page after page of it, I could have sung along with him. I think I dropped off at one stage. Anyway, finally he ground to a halt. So I laughed.'

'You laughed?' I said. I could think of nothing that would get further up Wright's bulbous nose.

'I didn't know what else to do, Jesmond. Yes, I laughed and I said something like, "Well, Peter, you've got me bang to rights, it's a fair cop" and held out my arms so he could whack the old cuffs on.'

'Did he realise you were joking, sir?' I asked. Hollis shook his head. 'I don't think he recognises jokes. Not officially, anyway. You remember those two I told you?'

'Yes, sir' I replied. 'Very risible.'

'Quite. Nary a titter from P. Wright though. "I don't see where the armadillo comes into it" was all he had to say. Anyway, to cut a long story short I said, "Peter, I am not a spy." I thanked him for being so frank, good to have a chat, and all that, and he left. And that was it. End of story, I hope. What's this?'

'I think, sir, that I've finally nailed the Fifth Man.'

'Oh, shit' said Hollis. His reaction surprised me.

'Don't you want to know who it is?' I asked.

'Not really' he said. He sounded very tired. 'Apart from anything else I've been firmly convinced for years that there is no such person. Indeed I have often thought that if anyone else came in here ranting on about High-level Penetration, I would do the decent thing and leave a loaded Luger in his office.'

He was flipping nervously away at the corner of my report. Then he took a deep breath.

'All right, Jesmond. This is conclusive proof, is it?'

'Absolute One Hundred Per Cent, sir.' I crossed my heart, and swore to die.

'Right.' He was smacking his lips together nervously and rolling his eyes in an agitated manner. Another enormous deep breath. 'Who is it?'

'Victor Rothschild' I barked.

'Fuck off!' he shouted, and threw my report out of the window.

There was a long silence. While Hollis recovered his basic breathing technique. It's one of those things we take for granted, and then comes a moment of stress, or panic: you forget to breathe out, or you keep breathing in, and the rhythm goes completely. I'd been thinking as I ran up the stairs that with Hollis retiring and Martin Funeral-Jones taking over, there would be posts to be filled by men of proven loyalty and inititiative – Deputy Director-General, for instance. Ah, well. That was the precise moment that I should have handed in my resignation.

'Have *you* thought of retiring?' said Hollis, restored at last.

I really meant to say 'Yes', I should have said 'Yes', my life would have been the fuller, the richer if I had said 'Yes'.

'No' I said.

And I carried on rapidly about soldiering on, doing my bit, keeping the home-fires burning and wished him a happy retirement, and fled. Yet another I would never see again.

HOUSE OF COMMONS
LONDON SW1A 0AA

Tuesday

I am the SPIDER! I
am the Centre of a huge web.
I may well ask you to go up
the Charing Cross Road and
whisper something or other in
a BLIND MAN's ear —
THEN kick him in the parts.

H. Wilson

This puzzle was solved within 30 minutes by 21% of the competitors at the 1987
Regional Final of the *Times* / London Rubber Company code-breaking championship.

12

1968. Well that's what it said on my calendar. I didn't care particularly. Hollis was gone. Wright was cleared. Rothschild wasn't a spy after all. And I don't think Funeral-Jones knew I existed. Mine was not a fat file. Hollis might have left a note. So I sat in my office and did the crossword. Then I'd rub it out and do it again. Then I'd make paper darts out of the paper, and that was it really. Mrs Beardmore had nothing for me. Well, coffee and a bun. Sometimes a fancy, but nothing I could work on or follow up. Even the view down the front of her overall had diminished sadly with the years. I was sitting there one morning, thinking that I might as well seize the moment and take to drink in earnest, when there was a knock at my door. I quickly unfolded my paper dart and pretended to read it.

'Come in' I shouted adding, 'Bloody Bulgars at it again. Looks like a job for Jesmond Barker' to impress whoever lurked without. Around the corner of the door came a white-haired, pasty-faced head not unlike a papier-mâché moose.

'I am not here' he said.

'Point taken' I replied.

He entered. A huge, baggy man. His body could have been that of a children's entertainer, but his face would have frightened the little blighter to bits. Moose? This is Raymond Chandler country surely. I am Philip Marlowe and this is the Moose, and he wants me to find his girl-friend. I put my feet up on the desk, and pulled half-a-bottle of Gordons out of a drawer, in an attempt to sustain the fantasy.

'Shay Shomething, feller, if it'sh only Farewell, My Lovely' I lisped in my best Bogart.

'You are Jesmond Barker?' asked the Moose.

'You shaid a mouthful, Shweetheart' I replied. These were the early symptoms I should have spotted.

'Cecil Harmsworth King' said the Moose.

'What a thing' said Philip Marlowe. 'Over to you, bison-breath' and he handed back to Jesmond Barker, who really wasn't ready for this.

'I've done my bit for MI5' said Cecil Harmsworth King. 'Hollis gave me your name. He said you were reliable and didn't have a lot to do.'

Thank *you*, Roger. So this is Cecil Harmsworth King. Supremo of the Mirror Group, the world's largest publishing empire? My word, *he* could be one of theirs.

'What do you think of Harold Wilson?' asked King, suddenly. Harold Wilson? Now he's one of theirs, isn't he? Rumours abounded along the corridors, and had done so ever since Hugh Gaitskell's untimely death.

'Are you for him, or against? Quickly, man.'

'I think he's a weasel' I said, non-committal to the last.

'You love your Country, Barker?'

'Almost' I replied, 'as much as gin.'

'Then you are the man for me. I want a trained man at my elbow, a man I can trust. We are on the brink of what History may view as the turning-point in our Country's fortunes. Join us, Barker, on the Long March.'

'*How* long' I enquired, for my legs have never been the same since the night under Wright's desk.

'I speak figuratively' he rapped. 'You are aware, of course, that up and down the land, small groups of dedicated men are banding together with the highly commendable intention of wresting the Country back from the Communists and Pinkoes into whose foul hands it has fallen?'

'Of course,' I lied. Somebody may well have told me, I probably wasn't listening. But if everybody else know, I was not going to appear ignorant.

'I personally know at least four retired Generals with men,

armed, and ready to march as far North as Warrington. The Army would quickly rally to our side. The City is waiting anxiously for us to act. We seize the Country, Barker, Captains of Industry move smoothly into the great offices of State. Strikers, henceforth, will be shot. Britain shall be Great again, Barker! Is this not the most exciting news you have ever heard?'

I was suddenly seized by a sudden and violent urge to break wind. This would not be the clarion-call he was anticipating. I clamped my buttocks firmly together. '*Ils ne passerant pas*' I said.

'Good man!' said King, 'and today I am approaching He Who I Hope Will Be Our Leader.' The capital letters crackled on his lips.

'And you want me to – er –?' I could not really envisage a role for myself in the Revolution.

'To be my personal security. You are armed?'

I can draw my fishing-tackle from the Quartermaster' I tapped the side of my nose. 'I'll say I'm on a case.'

'I'll pick you up outside Harrods in an hour. Welcome, Barker, to a Brave New World.' It must be hell to spend your life speaking in headlines. I was about to ask 'Which door?' but he had gone.

*　　*　　*

I had never met Funeral-Jones. I had seen him in the distance at the party they gave a few days after his appointment, but we had not been introduced. Given that the impression I received from King was that the Coup would be common knowledge to the Secret Service, I was surprised by Funeral-Jones' reaction.

'Oh God, that's all we need. Military coup sponsored by the KGB Bloody Red Army colonel marching on to *News At Ten*, shooting Alistair Burnet through the hair, pointing his pistol at the camera, and shouting "Hands up Britain! We are the Masters now!" Bang goes the pension, Jesmond.' He poured me a drink. I was even more confused than previously. I signalled for a large one myself.

'You say "Military coup sponsored by the KGB." I thought Cecil was one of ours.'

'*Is* he? I think you're right. He was very pro-Wilson at the Election, and the general feeling seems to be that Moscow ran *him*. This is bloody complicated, Barker. King's moved Right!

Those buggers always do. Look at Rothschild. I mean I can't stand that little rat Wilson, but KGB or not, he's PM, and I suppose we should rally to the Flag. We don't want Cecil Harmsworth King in Number Ten, do we?'

'I don't think that's the plan, sir. It's someone bigger. Cecil wouldn't name him, but he looked very pleased with himself'.

'Bigger' said Funeral-Jones. 'Bigger? Who can that be?'

'I'm meeting him' I looked at my watch, 'within the hour, whoever he is.'

'Well done, Barker' Funeral-Jones stood, and almost saluted, 'Then I can leave the whole thing in your hands. Good luck!'

I went downstairs to collect my .303 Lee Enfield. I felt very queasy.

★   ★   ★

I marched round and round Harrods very slowly with my fishing-tackle at the slope. Some forty-five minutes later, a Bentley glided up beside me.

'Ah, there you are' cried Cecil Harmsworth King from within. 'I'd forgotten what you looked like. Get in.' I got in. We drove to Kinnerton Street.

'His London home' said King, beaming proudly. We were ushered in by some sort of aide, who showed us into a book-lined study. The books at first glance seemed to be all nautical from *Masterman Ready* to *Jane's Fighting Ships*. King opened a cupboard full of charts and sea-going objects.

'Get in here' he said, 'listen hard, and keep the safety-catch off.'

My place in History would seem to be either under a desk or in a cupboard. I made myself comfortable, and thought about Harold Wilson. The rumour had been that Gaitskell had been injected with some little-known African virus by the KGB. No-one admittedly had ever been able to work out *how*. If at all. However, a defector, one Golitsia, told us that a contact in the Assassination Department (No. 13) of the KGB had told him that they were going to knock off a highly-placed European leader in order to get their man into office. It seemed most likely to be England. I felt they might already have assassinated Lord Home, it was hard to tell one way or the other, but it would point the finger at Edward Heath. Why not? Then again, if it *was* Gaitskell, for a while it seemed *George Brown* might succeed him. Whatever it had kept MI5 and P. Wright happy for some time investigating Wilson's trips to Moscow, and his East European friends, such as Lord Kagan, the Gannex raincoat man. Oh dear, I was boring myself to death in a strange cupboard. At last, action. People entering. I peeped through the crack and got the shock of my life.

All right, so I wasn't prepared for this. I began to judder. The strap of my Lee Enfield rattled against the butt. All those years in MI5 during which I had somehow managed to hang on to my marbles, while all round me were losing theirs, vanished down the drain. I mean some things are sacred, aren't they? And to see no less a person than Lord Mountbatten taking the chair at a meeting to discuss a Military Coup. Well, if the old brain is destined to snap, the will to live deserts you, then that's a good a moment as any.

I have no idea what they discussed. It sounded lively, but I was trying to have a major breakdown without disturbing anyone, and that required all my concentration. How long I stayed in that cupboard I do not know. I was woken by a thunderous bang as my rifle went off. I fell out of the cupboard. Lord Louis sat alone in front of a gas-fire studying a map of England covered in arrows and stars. A Man of Action, he showed little emotion as I staggered to my feet. I cannot imagine who, or what he thought I was. A strange white-faced man with wild eyes, toupee at a rakish tilt, twisted by cramp, armed with a Lee Enfield. I sloped arms stiffly and marched out of his life; shouting as I left,

'Don't do it, whatever it is! Lie down, and think of England!'

And in retrospect, he must have. Perhaps, just perhaps, he was sitting there gazing at the map, thinking all this could be mine, has not Cecil Harmsworth King so vowed. But, torn by doubts, on the one hand was he not descended from Charlemagne? Was he not a Man of Destiny? On the other, might he not be in the hands of raving loonies out on a spree? And as these thoughts battled in his tortured mind, might he not have been waiting for a sign? Might he not have made a serious error of judgement in thinking that *I* was that sign? That bizarre figure that sprang from nowhere with a massive bang represented all those Private Armies that paraded the Home Counties, shot to pieces by Harold Wilson's loyal Regulars? Might that not have given him cause to pause? Anyway, that was the end of that. I certainly wasn't going to advertise my part in it. When I got back to Leconfield House, I tidied myself up and went to see Funeral-Jones. I told him that I had been left waiting outside Harrods, and that King had obviously had doubts about my loyalty.

'Well, don't worry, old fellow' said the D-G. 'We'll keep an eye on it. We tend not to have revolutions in this country. Apathy, that's our strength.'

★   ★   ★

I sat at my desk for three days without moving. I told Miss Moneypenny I was not to be disturbed. Then in a brief moment of clarity that will sometimes come to one suffering from fatigue and malnutrition I wrote a large 'M' for Mountbatten on the wall opposite my desk. I sent Miss Moneypenny out for coloured chalks and began to write other names, some clearly, some in code, and to join them with different coloured lines, blue for our side, red for them, yellow for don't-knows, purple for possibles, green for doubles. Pink for gins too, I'm afraid. Sobriety would be no fit condition for a man whose brain had burst and was now taking one last final bash at the Great Conspiracy. It would be downhill all the way from now on.

Jesmond Barker Today.

13

The months went by, the pink gins slipped down, Wilson went, Heath came. Revolution didn't, Wright plodded on, Charlie Orange died. I had now covered every portion of wall in the office with names and links. If nothing else it was rather pretty, and it made sense to me. Almost everyone who was anyone was there. Mountbatten, Cecil King, Victor Rothschild (now in Heath's Think-Tank and still moving Right) Heath, Wilson, Brown, Maudling, most of the politicians of the day, City folk, Bishops, Publishers, Band-leaders, Professional Footballers, Pillars of Society, Authors, Actors, Painters and Decorators, Restauranteurs, Newspaper Proprietors, Jockeys – they were all linked for good or bad. Some had spread on to the floor, others were pinned to my desk. These had to be joined to the walls with coloured yarn. Chalks wouldn't work on carpet. There was Edward VII linked in yellow to the Kaiser, thence purple to Anthony Blunt and a note – 'Trip to Germany 1945'?

I would sit in my swivel-chair and swivel and marvel, and marvel further and swivel faster, but never so fast as to spill my pink drink, my constant prop. I loved my jigsaw. My superiors were not so keen. At first, they simply peeped round the door quickly, and fled. Then hints were dropped that I might like to take advantage of the Early Retirement Scheme. I sat in the middle of my psychedelic spiders' web and said, 'Not finished yet, sir, not finished yet.'

Then a Home Office Psychiatrist dropped in.

'There's still a piece missing,' I explained. He nodded. The whole thing seemed to make perfect sense to him. He plucked some of the coloured strings. He followed chalked lines with his finger. He expressed surprise at some of the names. He asked me who 'DUNGBEETLE' was. I pleaded the Official Secrets Act.

'Find that piece and you're home and dry' he said, and pausing as he left, suggested that I cut down on the pink gins.

'Righty ho,' I lied.

He ducked under several red strands and was gone.

Then, for the first time in my career in the Service, they gave me an assistant. Oh, I was not so potty that I didn't know he was a Watcher. He was one of the new breed. I remembered Blunt talking about the KGB's new breed after the War, when he spat out 'Bureaucrats' and 'Technocrats' – we had them now, nasty, common young men who talked nothing but 'shop' – through their noses. The Old Brigade, decent blokes whose loyalties extended beyond the Office, and their interests, were a dying breed. When I discovered he had worked under Wright for a year, my worst fears had been confirmed. He had loved every moment. His name was Colin Seaboot. Keen as mustard. Dull as cress.

'Still pursuing Roger Hollis to the grave, is he?' I enquired.

'Oh, yes, sir. He's still convinced. He said and I quote, "There's no escape for the man in the black suit playing golf in quiet retirement in the Somerset village of Calcott."'

'I don't suppose there are many people who play golf in black suits' I said. 'Undertakers, possibly. What's he up to at the moment?' It was a few years since I'd rifled through his office.

'Up to, sir? About here at the moment.' He gestured to his chin and laughed through his nose. 'He's been caught giving all the files on Wilson and Red infiltration into the Labour Party to Edward Heath and Co.'

'Oh, good.' I smiled happily.

'I think Victor Rothschild was behind it, sir. Anyway, all hell broke loose the length of Whitehall.'

'Excellent,' I said. I was enjoying this.

'They're not honouring his pension. MI5's policy now is that gentlemen's agreements are things of the past, and don't count any more. So, no pension, sir. Well, only a bit.'

'Wonderful' I said. I was beginning to like Colin Seaboot. He was the harbinger of the first glad tidings to come into my office for bloody years. I jotted down the latest information on the wall by his name. Purple lines sprang from his name like spikes on a sea anemone. Oh, joy! Oh, bliss!

★   ★   ★

Then to the embarrassment of MI5 at precisely the wrong moment, Harold Wilson and the Labour Party (bags of red and purple lines sprouting thence!) were returned as a minority government.

Seaboot came in one morning agog. I quite forgave him for ripping out all the red and blue thread linking Lord Gnome, Richard Ingrams, Bob Hope, James Goldsmith, the KGB, the MCC and the CIA, not that I'd ever work all that again, when he gave me the latest scuttle-butt.

It had occurred to a large number of MI5 officers that we were in possession of a massive amount of material that could easily be used to bring down Wilson's Government. Some thirty officers were in favour of leaking these documents about the Labour Cabinet in particular H. Wilson, to the Press, both at home and overseas. I wondered if I detected Cecil King's hand in this, he was, afterall, an old MI5 man and may have lost faith in his Generals. Better the new boys at MI5. It was the Zinoviev letter all over again. Seaboot was one of the thirty.

'We're trying to get Peter Wright to copy the files on the Gaitskell business and the rest of it. He has access to the D-G's safe. He's thinking about it. Isn't that great?'

I didn't think that I could appear before Wright in the same way that I had put the wind up Mountbatten. I doubt if he looked for signs. And certainly wouldn't pay much attention to a vision.

Next day, Seaboot told me, the officers were turning quite nasty because Wright was refusing to play along with them. He was afraid of losing the bit of pension that remained.

'They're calling him a cowardy-custard, sir, but he won't relent.'

'Don't worry he'll justify himself in the last chapter, I've no doubt. He'll chase poor Hollis beyond the grave.'

I went back to my walls. I had lines to chalk, thread to pin.

★ ★ ★

A year or so passed. Hollis died. Wright retired to Australia, but Rothschild would pay him a fat whack to come back and help my old friend Pincher's distant relative Chapman write the book pointing the finger at Hollis. It was a considerable assault course now to enter my office. Cleaners were banned, as was Miss Moneypenny, now too fat and clumsy; only Seaboot and I could reach the swivel chair without causing havoc. I had a faint suspicion that Seaboot had effected some repairs himself – there were some quite strange marriages. For instance, I found it hard to believe a Mafia link between the Pope and Denis Thatcher. And yet...

We were swivelling gently, Seaboot and I, for lack of space, I was obliged to sit on his knee, searching for that one last piece that would solve the riddle. To my chagrin, after all those years it was Seaboot who spotted it. He pointed at the large 'M', my starting-point so long ago. He pointed to the lines, a rich variety of hues, that extended in all directions like a peacock's tail. It was very beautiful. He pointed to the space. I hastily downed a large pink gin. I didn't want to start juddering again.

'That's it, isn't it?' cried Seaboot, excitedly, through his nose 'That's bloody it. Isn't it? Isn't it?'

'I think you've cracked it, Seaboot' I said, calmly. I still couldn't bring myself to call him Colin. 'If it's true, we will need technical back-up. If it's untrue, then you, Seaboot, are as mad as I, and we will retire together to the Home for Lunatic Intelligence Officers near Walsall. Perhaps they will let us keep the swivel chair.'

We stood up and faced each other. There was a bond that transcended the Generation Gap.

'Got a couple of pals downstairs, Seaboot, eager for the fray?'
'Yes, sir!'
'Tell them, there's bags of room for glory, boys.'
'Let's go for it, sir!'
'Good luck' I cried. 'Colin!' I could do it.

★ ★ ★

I controlled Operations from my Office. You could move in

it now quite freely. The lines, the threads were irrelevant, you could ignore them. I had taken over one wall with the information about The Target. I was absolutely certain we were right. On my desk was a large sheet of blank paper, two telephones and Miss Moneypenny, looking anxious. For some reason, she did not share our total confidence. The telephone rang twice. Then stopped.

I smiled at Miss Moneypenny. 'This'll be Colin.' The phone rang again. I picked it up.

'Sir?'

'Yes.'

'Is that you, sir?'

'Are you secure?'

'I think so.'

'Have you something to tell me?'

'Bad news, sir'

'Biggs and Ladbroke, sir'

'Yes.'

'They were tailing Target, sir.'

'Yes.'

'They lost her, sir.'

'Where was she last?'

'Trooping the Colour, sir.'

'I'll put out an All Cars. She may have made a run for it.'

'It gets worse, sir.' Seaboot was beginning to panic. 'The horse was picked up by Special Branch. The Pantomime Horse, sir. With Biggs and Ladbroke in it, sir.'

'Invoke the Eleventh Commandment.'

'What's that, sir?'

'Oh, shit!' I said, and put the 'phone down. The other 'phone rang. Miss Moneypenny answered it, whispered a 'Sir', and put her podgy hand over the mouthpiece and told me with tears in her eyes that I was wanted upstairs at once, if not sooner. I sighed deeply. So this was how it would be. Not with a bang, but with a wimp.

'Type me out a letter of resignation, Miss Moneypenny. I shall come in to clear up tomorrow. In the meantime if they want me I shall be at The Hot-Bed, Filth Street, Soho, W1. If Colonel Balls wants me, you think I'm in Central Africa. If Seaboot calls back, tell him to get into the Palace, into her bedroom, if necessary, and put the frighteners on her, tell her that we know her secret. If the Coldstreams nab him, he can pretend to be mad. Do you think I'll get enough from the book rights to get to Australia?'

She wasn't listening. She was crying her heart out. I put a hand gently on her shoulder.

'Oh God, Jesmond' she wept. 'I've tried to hide it all these years, but now I must tell you. I have loved as no other woman has ever loved a man since the moment I first laid on you. I'm sorry, but I had to tell you.'

She tore off my toupee and clasped it to her various bosoms.

'Don't, Moneypenny' I said. 'I've had enough bad news for one day' and bald as a coot, I walked out into Gower Street and the real world. I looked back at Leconfield House.

'Bastards!' I cried, and hailed a taxi. At least I'd got that right. It was drizzling.